S · T · E · P

Programme director

Howard Bagshaw

Writing team

Peter Branson
Tim Brotherhood
John Hindhaugh
Joan Morecroft
Chris Robotham
Jonathan Smith
Zosh Wall

Key stage

3

CORE

*The right of the
University of Cambridge
to print and sell
all manner of books
was granted by
Henry VIII in 1534.
The University has printed
and published continuously
since 1584.*

Cambridge University Press

Cambridge
New York   Port Chester
Melbourne   Sydney

Published by the Press Syndicate of the University of Cambridge
The Pitt Building, Trumpington Street, Cambridge CB2 1RP
10 Stamford Road, Oakleigh, Melbourne 3166, Australia

First published 1991

In association with Staffordshire County Council

Designed and produced by Gecko Limited, Bicester, Oxon.
Printed in Great Britain at the University Press, Cambridge

A catalogue record for this book is available from the British
Library.

ISBN 0 521 40635 8

Cover design by Jo Ridgeway

TP
94/14
£6.95

Contents

How to use this book

In the box below you will see what Design and Technology is all about. This isn't everything though. Design and Technology can be much wider than this. It can be a creative adventure through a very wide range of activities. We hope that you will be involved with this creative work as you go through parts of this book.

In this book you will find a number of different themes. Your teacher may often decide which theme you will be working in. Hopefully, you too will often be able to decide which parts of a theme you wish to follow.

In each theme there is a wide variety of projects — often set in different situations. Your teacher may give you a clearer picture as to how the various parts of the theme fit together. Some pages within each theme contain clearly set tasks. On others there are some fairly short activities and on some pages there are opportunities for longer projects. Other pages offer information and guidance.

Most pages refer you to the **Datafile**. The names of the sheets you might need from the Datafile are shown on each page. This Datafile should be available to you within your working area. Use it to collect information when you need it for your project. Your teacher may have other information available in the form of books, magazines, computer databases, etc., for you to use.

Think creatively and good luck!

What is Design and Technology all about?

What is Design and Technology all about?

It's about:
- responding to needs
- using materials
- balancing reasons for and against
- turning ideas into reality
- making decisions
- looking at products and ideas from other cultures and other times
- improving the quality of life
- attitudes and values
- economics
- industry
- imagination and creativity
- people and the environment
- improving things
- inventing
- flashes of inspiration
- making things
- applying knowledge
- fun

Action checklist

Have you thought about the following?

- Doing some research about needs and opportunities within a situation

- The possible effects of designing something to meet a need

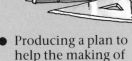

- Using drawings to express your ideas

- The reasons why you want to do this project

- Taking your brief/challenge and making a specification (i.e. the features of your design, e.g. materials to be used, sizes, costs, purpose, user, situation)

- Looking at other designs, including those from other times and cultures

- Using the good points from different designs to develop your ideas

- Producing a plan to help the making of your design go smoothly

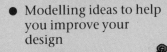

- Modelling ideas to help you improve your design

- Looking at your specification when evaluating your work

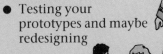

- Experimenting with different materials and equipment

- Testing your prototypes and maybe redesigning

- Asking other people for their opinions and advice

- Making a presentation of your evaluation

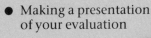

Hands on!

FOLIO DEVELOPMENT

CONTEXT

Next term children in the local primary school will be doing some work based on the theme 'Nursery rhymes and fairy stories'. The teacher would like you to illustrate a story with a puppet show using small finger puppets.

How many characters will I have in the story?

Size of finger/hand?

What sort of puppets are popular with children or adults?

What sort of stories do children like?

Do I need a script?

If I use card how strong will it need to be?

Where can I go for information that will help me?

Who can I ask?

Coming up with your design brief

Using no more than fifty words can you explain what you hope to produce in order to solve the problem?

Throughout this activity you will be asked to record your ideas and produce sketches and drawings illustrating the materials, characters and models you have decided to use. At every stage you must evaluate your work, improving or modifying it to ensure that the end result answers the brief you have set. You will be asked to present these drawings collected together in a portfolio.

This folio will be your record of your work and your thoughts. It will also help you and your teacher, as well as others, understand the way you solved the problems.

Research

Gathering information to help you

people in stories or rhymes look rather strange!

My favourite Story

The Happy family

The love sick frog

Children's favourite Tales

Stories or Rhymes
I could use one of the following stories or rhymes for my puppet show
1) Peter Pan
2) Robinson Crusoe
3) Babes in the wood
4) The big book of fairy tales
5) Mother Goose
6) Little red riding hood
From all the stories I have looked at these are my favourite

RESEARCH
Information that could help me

RESEARCH

If your puppet show is to be interesting and special you must choose a very good story or rhyme. You may also consider the following.

1 What types of characters feature in traditional puppet shows?

2 Why are certain puppets more popular than others? Will your show have a hero and/or a villain?

3 Television puppets are very popular with young children. Why are they popular? What special features do they have?

4 Are puppets new? Were puppets popular when your parents were young?

5 Can you find out from younger children which stories or rhymes they like best?

6 Do you need to research other things?

Can you produce a research page for your folio? This should help you understand the problem.

• D A T A   F I L E •
Research techniques
Sketching
Information systems

Ideas

THINK ABOUT

- characters
- location
- time of year
- dialects.

What other things are important?

Is your rhyme or story:

- exciting
- interesting
- unusual
- strange?

FOR YOUR STORY

During your research you may have discovered an unusual or interesting rhyme or story for the puppet show.

The Mad Professor
years ago in dark land
Old castle-high wall around
Five unhappy children
Mad inventor
Inventions never work
Magic spells
Growing Powder
Accidentally put
Two tall chill
seek help

The Mad Professor
Years ago in a dark unhappy land lived a mad
professor with five very unhappy children.
The castle had very high walls and no one
from the outside world ever came to visit.
One day a strange little goblin arrived and
promised to help the children escape to the
happy land. The goblin gave the professor a
secret menu telling him how to make growing
powder. One drop of growing powder and a
human would grow 30 cm.

What will your characters say?

◆

Will you need a script?

◆

How will the performance start and end?

◆

How many puppets will you need?

◆

Will your audience find your puppet show entertaining?

Can you give reasons for what you want to do?

Can you talk to others about the things you would like to do in your puppet show?

You may have to do some further research to give you ideas for things to design.

You may wish to use a computer to word-process your handwritten work.

IDEAS

Write out a quick draft of the story for your puppet show. You may need to include speech to make the story more realistic.

• DATA FILE •

Presentation techniques
Information systems

IDEAS

- Make a list of the puppets in your story. Can you draw the puppets showing various ideas for each one?

FOR YOUR CHARACTERS

Your research may have helped you with ideas for character and scenery.

Will you need drawings or pictures of other characters or 'props' for the story?

Can you describe your design ideas?

Can you give reasons why you have chosen a particular design?

Can you use drawings with comments on them to help you show your ideas for characters and scenery?

Ideas

FOR YOUR SCENERY

Can you use information from other times and cultures to help you with your ideas?

Can you choose suitable ideas for different parts of your puppet show?

IDEAS

- Can you imagine the setting or location of your story or rhyme? What scenery will be required? Can you illustrate these ideas in your folio?

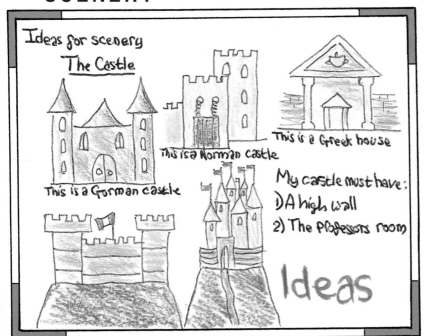

Will you change all or parts of the scenery? Can you use pictures from magazines or books?

Models

PUPPETS

Making models (prototypes) to
evaluate your ideas

THINK ABOUT

- size of your finger
- thickness of paper or card
- scale or proportion
- colours for effect
- different fixing systems

How can you include
information or results from
your model making in your
design folio?

Using paper, card or similar material
can you make models (prototypes) and
evaluate some of your ideas?

• D A T A F I L E •

Modelling
Sketching
Nets/developments

PUPPET THEATRE

Can you modify a cardboard box to form a puppet theatre? Can you model your ideas using a small box as a prototype?

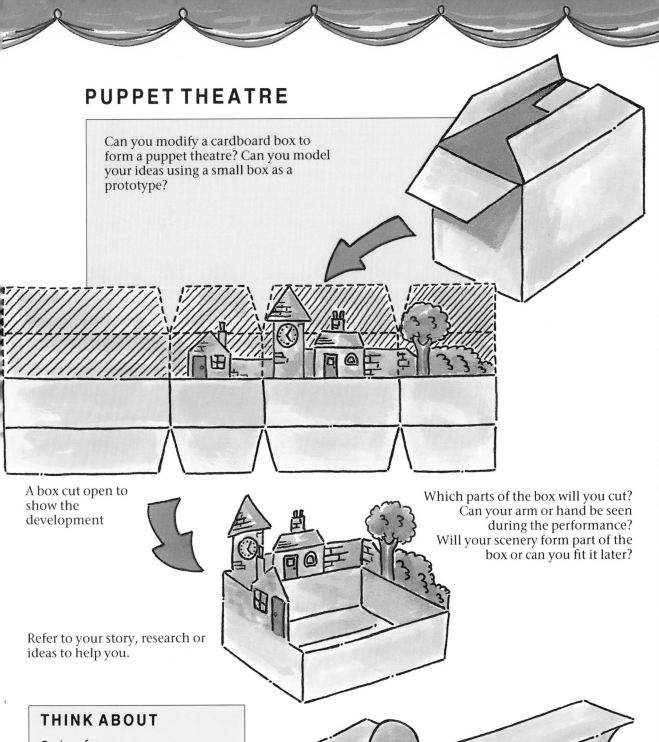

A box cut open to show the development

Which parts of the box will you cut? Can your arm or hand be seen during the performance? Will your scenery form part of the box or can you fit it later?

Refer to your story, research or ideas to help you.

THINK ABOUT

- size of stage
- distance of audience from theatre
- scale size of scenery
- changing the scene
- special effects
- electric lighting
- 3-D appearance

Evaluating

The folio pages will illustrate your final ideas and explain WHY you have chosen a particular design or material.

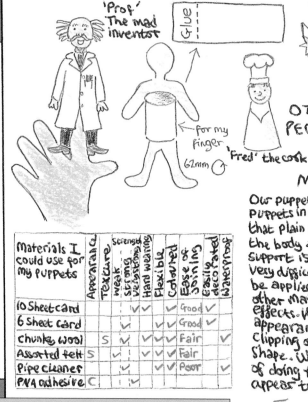

'Prof' The mad inventor

Glue

for my finger

62mm

'Rosy' The magic fairy

OTHER PEOPLE

'Fred' the cook

'Jolly' the witch Black wool

My Puppets

Our puppet show will have four puppets in the story. We have found that plain white card, 10 sheet for the body and 6 sheet for the finger support is the best. Thicker card is very difficult to cut. Colour will be applied using felt tips with other materials used to give special effects. We can change the appearance of the puppets by clipping other parts onto the body shape. We have tried different ways of doing this. Simple cardboard tags appear to be the best and quickest.

Materials I could use for my puppets	Appearance	Texture	Strength weak	Strength strong vibrations	Hard wearing	Flexible	Coloured	Ease of joining	Easily decorated	Waterproof
10 Sheet card				✓	✓			✓	Good	✓
6 Sheet card				✓				✓	Good	✓
Chunky wool	S	✓				✓	✓	Fair		✓
Assorted felt	S		✓		✓	✓	✓	Fair		
Pipe cleaner			✓			✓	✓	Poor		
PVA adhesive	C			✓						

Evaluating

EVALUATING YOUR MODELS

Your models and prototypes will help you decide on your final designs. Can you illustrate your ideas for the folio, indicating sizes, materials and other details you consider important.

THINK ABOUT

- Can you discuss how pleased you are with your work so far?
- How do your prototypes compare with what you set out to do?
- Have you made any important decisions during the project?
- Can you suggest some improvements to your designs?
- Can you say whether the needs you identified at the beginning were right?
- Do you need to record or develop ideas for other parts you will need for your puppet show?

Quite often illustrations and text in a folio can be produced on a computer or cut out and pasted using an adhesive stick.

Artfile books contain pictures, borders and illustrations you can photocopy and use in your folio.

• D A T A   F I L E •

Electrical circuits
Presentation techniques
Evaluating

Details

You will have to identify all the special effects or small parts required for your puppet show.

Small parts may be required.

Very small electric lights may be required to give effects such as day and night.

Small sketches, quick drawings and even things that don't work can be included in your folio. You may wish to cut things out and fix them onto a page using an adhesive stick.

Faces or clothing can be changed using clip-on shapes.

Sound effects can be made using common items found around the home or classroom. Records or tapes can provide special effects.

CHEER NOW!

BOO AND HISS NOW!

CLAP NOW!

You may need notices telling the audience what to do!

Planning
THE
PERFORMANCE

Will you need to amplify your voice?

Meet with others in your group and decide how to organise your puppet show.

Do you need to produce a programme?

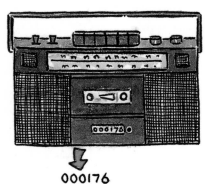

000176

A cassette recorder may be required to play sound effects.

Can you find different sound effects quickly during the performance?

Organize your time and resources for the performance

↓

Arrange room or hall for performance

↓

Check with primary school the numbers attending your performance

↓

Is room correct size?

Arrange another room or location

Arrange location in the room of puppet theatre and audience

↓

Can audience hear easily?

Arrange the use of a sound system with microphone

• D A T A   F I L E •

Flowcharts
Evaluating

FINAL
Evaluation

Now that you have completed your project can you say how pleased you are with your work? How well does it answer the brief you wrote at the beginning?

When you started this project a particular need had been identified for you. The Context on page 6 explained a teacher's need in the primary school. Can you say whether the needs you identified from the context were correct? What have you made to answer the different needs?

You will have used a range of materials such as paper or wool. Can you comment on how you have used these materials? Could you use them more effectively next time?

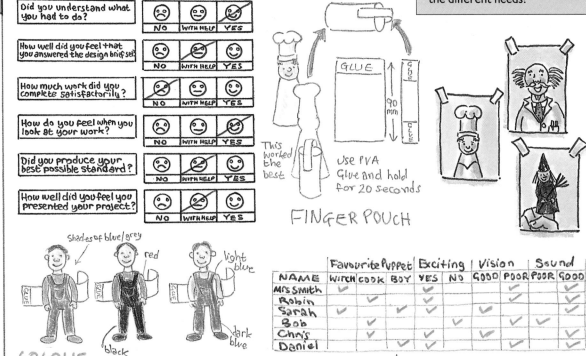

Did you understand what you had to do? — NO / WITH HELP / YES

How well did you feel that you answered the design brief set? — NO / WITH HELP / YES

How much work did you complete satisfactorily? — NO / WITH HELP / YES

How do you feel when you look at your work? — NO / WITH HELP / YES

Did you produce your best possible standard? — NO / WITH HELP / YES

How well did you feel you presented your project? — NO / WITH HELP / YES

Shades of blue/grey
red
light blue
dark blue
black
COLOUR

GLUE
90 mm
This worked the best
Use PVA Glue and hold for 20 seconds
FINGER POUCH

NAME	Favourite Puppet			Exciting		Vision		Sound	
	WITCH	COOK	BOY	YES	NO	GOOD	POOR	POOR	GOOD
Mrs Smith	✓			✓			✓		✓
Robin				✓					
Sarah	✓		✓	✓		✓			✓
Bob		✓			✓		✓	✓	
Chris		✓		✓			✓		✓
Daniel		✓		✓		✓			✓

Evaluation

You may have asked some of the children or teachers in the audience what they think about your puppet show, questions such as:

Did they enjoy it?

Could they hear clearly?

Did they like some puppets more than others?

Was the story exciting and interesting?

Can you make a presentation of your evaluation?

LITTLE ◆ SNORING TIMES

Leisure

HOLIDAYS

SUN & SAND

Australia
Beaches
Florida
Greece
Mediterranean

THEME

Whodunnit

TOURING

B & B
Caravanning
Coach tours
Cycling

WATER SPORTS

Diving
Sailing
Water skiing

WILDLIFE

Nature rambles

WINTER SPORTS

Skating
Skiing
Hiking

ADVENTURE

Biking
Hiking
Safari
Walking

CULTURAL

Educational
Heritage tours
Historical

CINEMA

Films
Actors
Actresses
Adventure
Thrillers
Science fiction
Travel

COLLECTING

Bicycles
China
Cuddly toys
Dolls
Flowers of the world
Fossils
Key rings
Model cars
OO & N Gauge trains
Pebbles
Stickers

CRAFTS

Basket making
Glass engraving
Knitting
Tatting
Weaving
Woodturning
Stained glass

HOBBIES

Bird watching
Train spotting
Gardening
Do-it-yourself
Music
Painting
Sport

• DATA FILE •

Research techniques
Presenting information
Presentation techniques

Play Spot the Ball

C L A S S I F I E D

COLLECT...

as much information as possible on different types of holidays. Do not confine yourself to common types of holiday, look for the more unusual as well.

You might like to ask people:

- what sort of holidays they have been on
- how they travelled
- what sports they take part in
- what sights they enjoy visiting
- what entertainment they like
- how they choose their accommodation
- what their holidays cost.

Some places and people to help with information are:

- tourist information centres
- Tourist Boards
- travel agents
- libraries.

Where else will you find information? This page should give you an idea.

Present the information you have gathered properly. This might involve writing up your conclusions using a word processor or drawing graphs to indicate the popularity of different holidays.

The cost of various holidays may be interesting to compare. Is there a computer program available to make this comparison easier?

i

HOLIDAYS

A vast number of holidays are available. Everything from lightweight hiking trips to year-long round-the-world cruises. Methods of transport vary greatly. Package holidays can be by air, coach, rail or car, or the more leisurely camping & caravanning short breaks.

The emphasis of some holidays is on creative pursuits such as painting, crafts or voluntary work.

Sport holidays are more and more popular and include

- tennis
- squash
- athletics
- golf
- skiing

Canals are attracting more and more visitors, with specialist companies even offering horse-drawn narrow boats. Some travel firms offer country touring holidays by car, minibus or bicycle. The lists are almost endless. Activity and hobby holidays are popular and some of them do useful work for charities or conservation causes.

Have you thought about the ways in which you can gather information on holidays? Collect some examples to see the type of information given. From the investigations you carry out define the various types of holiday on offer.

There are also different ways to travel while on holiday. You could do a survey by asking your friends and family to think of the advantages and disadvantages of any particular method of transport.

What type of activities do people want to be provided on a holiday? See if you can find even more.

Record all the information you collect. By brainstorming identify a promotional item to sell a holiday which interests you such as a tea-towel or teddy-bear skier.

You now have the information to design and produce a prototype promotional item for a leisure activity of your choice. Your outcome may well be restricted by some or all of the following:

- expertise
- resources
- time.

• D A T A   F I L E •

Research techniques
Presenting information
Brainstorming

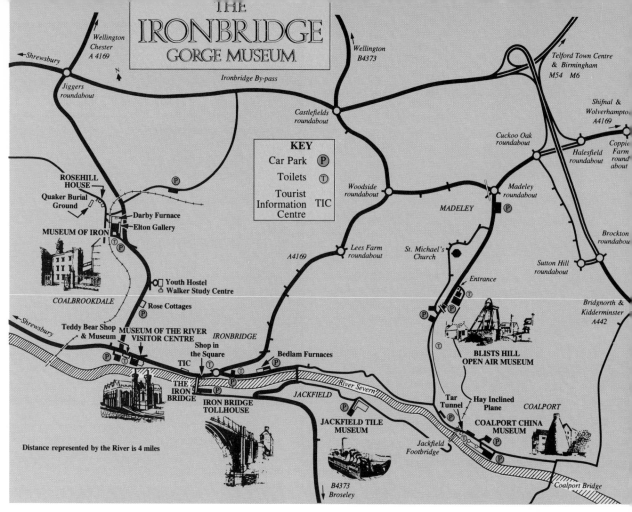

THE
IRONBRIDGE
GORGE MUSEUM

Ironbridge By-pass

KEY

Car Park   Ⓟ

Toilets   Ⓣ

Tourist
Information   TIC
Centre

Shrewsbury
Wellington Chester A 4169
Jiggers roundabout
Wellington B4373
Castlefields roundabout
Telford Town Centre & Birmingham M54 M6
Shifnal & Wolverhampton A4169
Cuckoo Oak roundabout
Halesfield roundabout
Coppice Farm roundabout
Woodside roundabout
Madeley roundabout
MADELEY
Brockton roundabout

ROSEHILL HOUSE
Quaker Burial Ground
Darby Furnace
Elton Gallery
MUSEUM OF IRON

A4169
Lees Farm roundabout
St. Michael's Church
Sutton Hill roundabout

Youth Hostel
Walker Study Centre
COALBROOKDALE
Rose Cottages

Entrance
Bridgnorth & Kidderminster A442

Shrewsbury
Teddy Bear Shop & Museum
MUSEUM OF THE RIVER VISITOR CENTRE
Shop in the Square
IRONBRIDGE
Bedlam Furnaces
BLISTS HILL OPEN AIR MUSEUM

TIC
THE IRON BRIDGE
IRON BRIDGE TOLLHOUSE
JACKFIELD
River Severn
Tar Tunnel
Hay Inclined Plane
COALPORT

JACKFIELD TILE MUSEUM
Jackfield Footbridge
COALPORT CHINA MUSEUM

Distance represented by the River is 4 miles

B4373 Broseley
Coalport Bridge

TOUR GUIDE

The leisure industry has grown considerably in the last twenty years. Why do you think this is? There are many possible reasons. See if you can come up with a list of these after discussion.

Many leisure attractions are meant to entertain visitors for quite long periods of time. Is it important that visitors can find their way around effectively? What are the different ways this is achieved? Give specific examples from your own experience. Are there occasions when several different methods could be used together?

Think about people who may have particular difficulties with some of the suggested methods. For example, children, the elderly, blind or partially sighted, people confined to wheelchairs.

Design your own information system for a specific leisure activity. You will need detailed information about it and as much information about the things on offer there as possible.

The information on this page has been collected from the Ironbridge Gorge Museum Trust. You may want to design an information system for one of the sites.

A simple system might involve an A4 folded leaflet giving basic information. This is only one method. See if you can design one of your own.

Severn Warehouse, Ironbridge, erected in the 1840s. ▲

Aerial view of the Ironbridge Gorge. ▽

THINK ABOUT

- Space is likely to be limited. Consider carefully the essential information and exclude other potentially confusing information.

- 'A picture paints a thousand words'.

- Some people may not be able to read a 'flat' plan.

- Don't try to do too many things at a time; e.g. are you directing people *to* the site, or *around* the site once they have arrived?

• DATA FILE •
Brainstorming
Presentation techniques

Investigate the ways in which organisations promote themselves. This could be through regular advertising of many kinds; for example, appearing in television programmes either through regular features such as Telethon, Tomorrow's World or The Clothes Show, or as part of a news item.

Collect and display information about promotional items, including the actual artefacts where appropriate.

Many promotional items are associated with leisure activities and attractions.

promo

Alton Towers is a large theme park in Staffordshire and below are listed just a few of the promotional items on sale in the park.

Ties, badges, mugs, key fobs, pens, T-shirts, flags, car stickers, bookmarks, pencils, carrier bags, paper weights, writing pads, aprons, sunglasses, hats, erasers.

Some people enjoy taking a souvenir home from trips. Something which is special to the place visited is often chosen, perhaps a mug with 'Alton Towers' on it. This is meant to be a constant reminder during everyday life of the fun and excitement to be had. Think carefully about the marketing strategies behind the concept of souvenirs.

Is the constant reminder likely to encourage you to return? Will other people see your souvenir and be influenced by it?

Does the park advertise? If so, does it have to pay for this? Are you paying for the privilege of advertising something you have paid to attend?

tional ITEM

Discuss the ways companies advertise without directly paying. Consider:

- sponsorship
- designer clothes
- limited edition articles
- letters of commendation
- famous people endorsing products.

Look again at the promotional items you collected earlier. Evaluate them by weighing up the information they give and investigating the way they are produced, not forgetting the marketing strategies that lie behind their production.

> You should now have enough information to design and make a promotional artefact for a local industry, leisure complex or site of historical interest.

The public expects a very high quality product at competitive prices. These two aspects should be high on your list of design considerations.

Investigate the use of IT techniques to produce high quality text and graphics.

You may need to try out different methods of printing designs onto a variety of materials, e.g. fabric, paper, ceramics, plastics.

• D A T A   F I L E •

Logos, signs and symbols
Lettering
Presentation techniques
Printing techniques

Alton Towers is set in 500 acres of the Staffordshire countryside and offers an enormous variety of activities for visitors, some of which are shown on this page. With so many people visiting the park many problems could arise. You may have experienced problems yourself. Visitors will return in the future only if they feel they have had value for money. It requires constant effort to keep the park running smoothly.

White knuckle rides are an important part of theme parks. They are always on the lookout for new ones. Have you got any good ideas?

Theme
PARK

Traditional fairs charge for each ride individually whereas Alton Towers and many other theme parks have a once-only admission charge which covers all rides in the park for that day. Both of these methods have disadvantages which other systems of charging could overcome. For instance control systems exist which might be used to monitor visitors. Phone cards have a magnetic strip with an initial value. This gradually reduces as the time units are used up. Could a similar system be used for visitors? How would this work?

Many of the shops and stalls are run by small businesses who pay rent for the opportunity to operate at Alton Towers. Can you think of any further opportunities? American's have a craze for frozen yoghurt! It may sound awful but it tastes like real ice cream and is far less fattening. Any ideas need to be fully documented and a business plan prepared. Do you know what is involved in presenting a business plan? Banks only offer loans for ideas which have a good chance of success. This usually involves showing them an example of the final product. A prototype is usually sufficient.

The Grand Parade each afternoon is a good crowd puller, but new floats are always needed to keep the show fresh.

It is important to offer a wide variety of food and refreshments for visitors.

Cheeky characters operate in an area called The Street. These are a favourite of the children who come to Alton Towers. They are never lost for words and always entertain.

Some visitors have trouble finding their way around despite being given a map of the site. Other systems might help such as signposting. Can you help?

All visitors arrive by the same entrance. This leads to bottlenecks at certain times of the day. Some of the furthest parts of the park are not full until well into the morning. Could visitors be shown where the shortest queues are for the rides? The technology exists to monitor the flow of people around the park and passing through each ride. Could this information be used to update a display of the whole park, or is there a better system?

Car parking is some way away from the park entrance. A futuristic monorail transports passengers from there to the amusements. This journey time is an ideal opportunity to inform people about the attractions in the park. This is not done at the moment. Can you think of an appropriate system? Information technology may offer exciting opportunities here.

Recently Alton Towers has diversified into special attractions. A recent pop concert attracted large numbers, and November 5th fireworks and laser shows are planned. The park includes extensive grounds and a mansion which is partly occupied and partly a restored ruin. These could form the basis of special events.

'Whodunit breaks' for Sherlock Holmes fans, or jousting competitions are just two undeveloped opportunities. Can you think of others?
A new attraction is the farm which operates as a commercial venture but is specially designed for visitors. Are there opportunities here to develop other themes?

Heritage centres preserve and display old-fashioned industries. The general public may already know about these twilight industries, but how much do they know about modern industries and technology? Would electronics or bio-fermentation make a suitable theme centre? Can you think of others? When the weather is bad there are a number of indoor areas but they are not as plentiful as the owners would like. They already have an arcade that they welcome new ideas for. Other opportunities for design and technology are identified in the next few pages.

REFRESHING
Ideas

STEP HIGH SCHOOL NOTICES

Educational Visit

STEP HIGHSCHOOL

£15 SIGN BELOW

Susan Smith
MARK THOMPSON   Bimla Patel
Jenny Brown   Rebecca Jones
Carol Newton   DAVID HEALY
Ranjit Sondh   Robert Truman
Tony May   Mary Wilson

If you were going on the above trip what would you like to eat? What drinks would you take? Remember you will have to carry everything.

POINTS TO CONSIDER

- 5–10 hours from preparation to eating
- carrying
- cost
- energy value
- keeping things cool/warm
- likes and dislikes
- nutritional value
- queasy rating!
- variety of tastes and textures

The choice between taking food or buying it there is not an easy one to make. The following stages will help you make this decision in an objective way.

What are the choices available at your destination? You will need to collect menus.

Given a free choice, with no restrictions, what would you choose from the menus? What would you take along to eat if you preferred a packed lunch? Don't forget to include drinks in your choice.

I FOR THOSE *Taking* FOOD:

Analyse your choices against the following factors:

- storage
- carriage
- preparation
- nutritional value
- cost
- environmental impact
- where food will be eaten.

This analysis should provide you with a clear idea about your first choice of food. You may wish to modify your choice to take account of these factors. Before trying out your ideas you should analyse what is involved.

At this point it is necessary to produce samples of the food you are likely to take with you so that a

2 FOR THOSE *Buying* FOOD:

Analyse your choices against the following factors:

- cost including
    - staff
    - premises
    - ingredients
    - cooking them
- queasy rating!
- nutritional value
- environmental impact
- where food will be eaten.

Your analysis will provide you with details which may make you reconsider your first choice. This is an opportunity to change your mind and choose a different menu for the day.
If you have made a new selection for your menu, a detailed analysis

should be done in the same way that you did for your initial choice. This analysis should be used as a comparison with the one made by pupils taking food of their own.

Ideally you should now carry out a taste test on the selected menu. This is not likely to be possible. Any comparison against food taken by the other group has to apply to factors on both lists.

taste test can be carried out. The following should feature in any tests you carry out:

- appearance
- carriage and condition
- packaging
- texture
- flavour
- waste in production
- economy of ingredients.

The information gained from the testing should be combined with the information from planning and producing the food to provide a comprehensive evaluation of your chosen menu. Be very careful to separate out factual information from personal likes and dislikes. Both are valid but the two should not be mixed up.

Your final results and analysis should allow you to compare your choices against those of the group buying food. The other group are not likely to be able to carry out a taste test.

3 COMBINED OUTCOME

- DATA FILE -

Nutritional guidelines

It should now be possible to produce a league table of preferences which could include aspects covered by your analysis and testing.

WHITE KNUCKLE RIDE

V isitors to Alton Towers constantly demand different and more thrilling rides. Existing rides include:

- Log Flume
- Grand Canyon Rapids
- Corkscrew
- Mouse
- Black Hole
- Pirate Ship
- Thunder Looper

Each ride has its own special attraction although people often find it difficult to explain what it is they like most.

Water forms a major part of some rides and usually adds to the spectacle and excitement.

A common feature of most white knuckle rides includes subjecting people to various amounts of G-force.

Corkscrew

Log flume

S peed itself does not thrill the most. (Few rides travel at more than 45 kph.)

Many of the rides use gravity to complete the ride once a motor has carried the carriages up to a high point. The classic roller coaster is a good example of this.

Can you devise a new white knuckle ride? Some of the factors which need to be considered when designing mechanical devices are listed below. The list is not meant to be comprehensive because different sets of criteria apply to the variety of possible solutions.

- G-force
- incline
- brakes
- sensors
- velocity
- potential energy
- kinetic energy
- friction
- structure
- mass
- time

Construction kits could provide a means of trying out ideas rapidly. Many toys such as trains or car racing sets may have tracks which could be useful for roller coaster type rides.

Electronic systems kits allow rapid modelling of control systems and have the advantage of being supported by several methods of realisation.

Safety on the real rides is of prime importance. This should also form an important factor in your designs. The rides must be strong enough to support a lot more than the expected load in each car.

Another important safety concept is 'fail safe'. You may need to investigate this aspect in more detail in order to evaluate your own designs.

The two major costs to running rides of this type are labour costs and energy consumption.

Labour costs can be reduced through the use of high levels of automation. The existing rides are surprising in their reliance on a high degree of manual control. In your design you could identify areas where alternative approaches are possible and justify your choice of manual or automatic control.

Energy consumption is fairly straightforward. The means to reduce it are, however, very diverse. Any design should be assessed for energy consumption and efficiency. In your testing and development work increasing efficiency should be a high priority.

Pirate ship

$$\text{Efficiency} = \frac{\text{energy output}}{\text{energy input}}$$

Remember that the fun factor is a major aspect of these rides. It is also the most difficult to quantify!

Black hole

• D A T A   F I L E •

Structures
Movement
Control systems

29

E ach day at 3 o'clock a Grand Parade takes place around Alton Towers. Several floats are driven around, each one based on a theme.

The pictures show some of the existing floats which can be seen at Alton Towers.

The floats are all built onto a standard milk float chassis. This makes them quiet and very stable because of the heavy batteries. All floats are the same overall size to aid storage.

Based on a standard size chassis and within the limitations of maximum superstructure dimensions, can you design an exciting float to include in the Grand Parade?

It is important that all your designs are to the same scale so that direct comparisons can be made. Your designs could also be based on the same rolling platform design.

Carnival productions rely very heavily on fabrics in the form of costumes and sets. Masks can also provide atmosphere.

There are opportunities here for you to be artistic in a sculptural way to create a float. Modelling materials such as clay, foam or papier mâché may be available.

GRAND

PARADE

The appearance of the float could also incorporate simple moving elements. Can you think of ways of making the forward movement of the vehicle operate the moving features you have designed?

Sound forms a vital part of traditional fairgrounds. This might make your float more appealing. How could you incorporate this?

Lights are also common features at fairgrounds. New techniques are being developed all the time and you may be able to think of techniques from other situations such as discos and pop concerts which could be useful here.

CAN YOU FILL THIS SPACE WITH AN AMUSING AND ENTERTAINING FLOAT DESIGN?

250mm

150mm

MAXIMUM HEIGHT 150mm

Use these dimensions to model your float.

• D A T A   F I L E •

Making
Modelling
Movement

ARCADE *ACTION*

Amusement arcades feature in towns and on motorway services as well as in leisure parks such as Alton Towers.

Most of the attractions centre around video games but occasionally there are other types such as the crane in the cabinet illustrated. Machines like this combine an element of skill with a modicum of luck giving the user a chance to win a cuddly teddy bear.

The chances of winning are affected by the way the bears are stacked in the cabinet and the way they are picked up by the grab. A set amount of time is allowed to position and pick up a bear. At the end of the alloted time wherever the grab is, it automatically returns to the chute and deposits whatever is in its grasp down the chute to be collected.

This activity focuses on just such an attraction. The owners of these amusements would like to extend the range of toys offered. The makers, however, are only able to supply teddies.

Can you design and make an alternative soft toy to the teddy bear for the cabinet? It must be of the sizes and weights specified in order to work with the machines which are already installed.

As with all toys intended for young children anything produced must conform to the appropriate safety standards.

You need to research this aspect very carefully before you begin your designs.

The cost of these amusements is usually quite low, about 50p being typical. This does not leave a very large margin to be divided among materials, running costs and profit. Any design must therefore feature material and production costs very high on its list of considerations.

Inspiration for new characters could come from traditional fairy tales, science fiction stories or from your own imagination.

Many of the cartoon characters which have appeared recently have been based on adventures or combat themes which involve violence. Even though many of the characters are fighting in the interests of justice many people are concerned about increasing violence in childrens' toys. Be careful to consider this aspect in your designs.

• D A T A   F I L E •
Fabric patterns
Joining
British standards

WIN! WIN!

STREET
Attractions

Cartoon type characters are commonly used for promotional and entertainment purposes.

Characters are often safety education in schools, and the fire brigade has a character called Welliphant.

Alton Towers has Pippin and Splodge who perform in the street part of the leisure park.

Pippin is a small van built on a golf-cart chassis. The human operator is hidden in the back of the van. He or she drives the van with both legs and one arm while the other arm operates the head of the character.

A headset allows the operator to hear and talk to the public outside the van. He or she can see through a dark mesh screen and cannot therefore be seen from outside.

Splodge is the size of a ten-year-old child and is radio controlled from some distance away. Its head turns from side to side and it can move forwards, backwards, left and right. The mouth moves in sync with the operator's voice when he is talking to people through a radio link.

Alton Towers would like to extend the range of characters and you are being given the task of designing a new personality. Can you produce a prototype of your design?

Outcomes to this challenge might range from simple puppets of different types controlled directly by human operators, to remote control characters like Splodge.

The time you need to complete this project will expand according to its complexity. With careful design a simple puppet with a human operator could be more effective than an automatic robot.

The aim is to interest and entertain the public, especially children.

The 'Think about' list should be looked at very carefully. A simple outcome, if made to work quickly, can always have extra features built in. There is nothing worse, however, than a complex project which is not finished and fails to work because insufficient time was available.

THINK ABOUT:

- keeping your designs simple and making them well
- creating only one or two 'actions' to begin with
- trying to appeal to both boys and girls
- alternative methods of providing movement and researching them thoroughly
- using the Datafile to identify a wide range of alternative control techniques
- exploring the alternatives thoroughly before fixing your design.

• DATA FILE •

Movement
Materials
Control systems

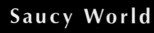

SAUCY WORLD

Interest in food from other countries has increased in recent years mainly as a result of travel abroad, the growth of the European Community and our multi-cultural society. In our neighbourhoods we have seen the introduction of specialist shops selling foreign food ingredients and specialist restaurants serving foods from other countries. Our meals could well be made up of dishes from a variety of countries.

Discuss this within your group and draw up a list of the types of foods they have experience of. Can they identify the country of source?

There has been an increase in public demand for easy ways of reproducing these dishes. The result is a wealth of convenience sauces – packets, jars, tins or frozen – which just need to be added to a basic list of ingredients to make the dish you want.

Look at the three different recipes shown here, each one representing foods from a different culture. Use one of these to carry out a detailed evaluation of such convenience foods. If you do not wish to make any of the dishes suggested choose a different type of convenience sauce and evaluate that.

Working in pairs plan your work together. Make the same dish but use a different make/type of sauce, e.g. compare a packet to a tin perhaps.

Throughout your work you will need to present your results, so you need to decide how best to do this before you start. The Datafile will help with suggestions.

Some of the areas you will need to look at are:

- nutritional value
- costings
- ease of making
- taste and texture
- authenticity.

Homepride
Classic Curry Sauce
ROGAN JOSH
"Medium spiced, with tomatoes, red and green peppers"

Rogan Josh gets its name from its mouthwatering warm, red appearance. Rich with tomatoes, subtly spiced but quite mild, it is a classic dish from the hills of Kashmir-now popular all over India.
Meat cooked in Rogan Josh is tender, spicy and full of flavour with a delicate aroma that is hard to resist.
HOW TO COOK For 4 portions of Lamb (or Beef) Rogan Josh, cut 450g (1lb) of uncooked meat into cubes and place in a casserole. Pour the Rogan Josh sauce over the meat and cook, covered, in a moderate oven (180°C/350°F/Gas Mark 4) for about 2 hours or until the meat is tender. Stir occasionally. Pre-cooked meat can be re-heated in the Rogan Josh sauce, simmer on top into cubes and mix with the curry sauce, simmer on top of the stove over a low heat for about 20 minutes, stirring occasionally.
WHAT TO SERVE WITH ROGAN JOSH Plain boiled rice is the classic accompaniment but with Indian meals other side dishes are important and carefully chosen to complement the flavours of the main dish. Try crisp green salad, a salad of sweetcorn and peppers, hot green beans or baked aubergines. And poppadums of course!
ONCE OPENED - the contents of the can will keep in a covered container in the refrigerator for 2-3 days. The sauce may also be frozen, cooked or uncooked, for up to 2 months.

383 g

BEST BEFORE END
OCT 92
110602

Colman's
Sauce

Spaghetti Bolognese
Sauce Mix
Colman's Spaghetti Bolognese Sauce Mix is the special ingredient for Spaghetti Bolognese and a whole range of Italian dishes. It's really tasty poured straight over mince, spaghetti or any pasta. And it's so easy to make!

Mixing Instructions
1 Pour ½ pint of water into a saucepan.
2 Add contents of the sachet and mix well.
3 Bring to the boil, stirring continually.
4 Simmer for 1 – 2 minutes.

Ingredients you will need for
Spaghetti Bolognese
1 lb minced beef
1 onion, chopped
4 oz mushrooms, sliced
1 packet of Colman's Spaghetti Bolognese Sauce Mix
½ pint water
Cooking oil

Brown the mince and onion in a little oil, drain off excess fat. Add the mushrooms, the contents of the sachet and the water, stir well. Bring to the boil, stirring continually, then cover and simmer for 20 minutes. Stir occasionally. Serve with spaghetti (or other pasta), and parmesan cheese.

NUTRITION INFORMATION: 100g provide
Energy	1356kJ/319 kcal
Protein	8.7g
Carbohydrate	69 g
Fat	1.0g

NO ADDED ARTIFICIAL COLO
OR ADDED PRESERVATIVES
INGREDIENTS: DRIED TOMATO, FLOUR, CORNFLOUR, SUGAR, SAL ONION, HYDROLYSED VEGETABL PROTEIN, FLAVOUR ENHANCER (SODIUM GLUTAMATE), CITRIC ACID, FLAVOURINGS, SPICES, PARSLEY, OREGANO.

By appointment to
Her Majesty Queen Elizabeth II
Manufacturers of
Mustards and Sauces
Colman's of Norwich

Colman's

40 g ℮

Carrow, Norwich, NR1 2DD.
Exported by Reckitt & Colman (Overseas) Ltd.,
Norwich, England.
Made in B

With this sauce you can quickly create an authentic Chinese dish as good as you will find in any restaurant. Sharwood's have used the finest ingredients to give a classic sweet and sour flavour.

Sweet and Sour Pork Stir Fry

Ingredients:
Serves 3-4
350g (12oz) pork – sliced thinly across the grain
1 x 15ml spoon (1 Tbsp) oil
225g (8oz) small carrots and green pepper – sliced to a similar shape and size as the pork
1 x 225g (8oz) can sliced pineapple – drained and chopped into cubes
1 bottle Sharwood's Sweet & Sour Sauce

Refrigerate after opening.
Rapidly fry the pork for 2-3 minutes in 1 x 15ml (1 Tbsp) oil, stirring continuously. Add the vegetables, continue stir frying for a further minute. Add pineapple cubes and sauce and heat through gently coating the ingredients thoroughly. Serve immediately.
For more recipes and information write to Dept SFS, The Chinese Kitchen, at the address shown.

J. A. SHARWOOD & CO. LTD.,
LONDON NW10 6NU
ENGLAND

INGREDIENTS:
Sugar, Vinegar, Lemon Juice, Water, Onions, Ginger, Modified Cornflour, Salt, Carrots, Pepper, Colour (E110).
FREE FROM ARTIFICIAL FLAVOURINGS.

5 00019 575874

• DATA FILE •
Presenting information

Making and trying the dish

First, using the ingredients listed on the sauce packaging and those you need to add to complete the dish work out its nutritional value. How many people will it serve? Use food tables to help with this.

Coq au vin ingredients	protein	fat	carbohydrates	vitamins A B C D	fibre	mine iron
Chicken						
Mushroom						
Onion						
Sauce						

It may be that the sauce you use claims to contain NO artificial additives or colourings. Why is it seen to be necessary to use these in convenience foods? Find out which ones are commonly used in sauces and what their function is.

Purchase the necessary ingredients to make your chosen dish remembering to keep a record of their cost.

It may be a useful exercise to research how easy it would be to obtain the necessary herbs and spices if you wished to make your own sauce.

Between you, draw up a plan for the making process and some means of recording points or comments you wish to make note of while you are working.

To enable you to ask others to help in the evaluation it may be useful to give them a list of suggested descriptions to summarise their opinions. What do you want them to comment on?

APPEARANCE
attractive/messy/colourful/appetising/neat/interesting

SMELL
spicy/sweet/sour/acid/oily/fruity/musty/mouthwatering

TASTE
spicy hot/insipid/highly-seasoned/sweet/sour/greasy/bitter

TEXTURE
soggy/crisp/al dente/firm/soft/crumbly/cold/set/runny

Following any instructions given on the packaging make the dish noting carefully the ease of making it and the clarity of any given instruction. Note any problems as you progress. Remember to time the different sections of the making process.

Carry out the evaluation of the completed dishes as soon as they are made. How do they compare with each other in all aspects – appearance, amount, flavour, texture, etc? Ask the opinion of others in your group as well as those at home.

Draw together and summarise all your comments and results and record them in a suitable manner. Discuss these with your partner and decide if there is any way in which this dish could be improved. How successful do you and others think it was?

Are there any alterations you would make to:

● contents of the sauce/add extra ingredients
● instructions for making on the packaging
● nutritional information on the packaging
● general appearance of the packaging?

Record and illustrate your suggestions.

THINK ABOUT

● Have you recorded your own thoughts?
● Have you discussed them with others?
● Have you thought of ways of collecting the opinions of others?
● Have you looked at existing designs?
● Have you looked at designs of the past and of other cultures?
● Have you evaluated your work against your specification?
● Have you considered the implications of your designs on others?
● Have you met the need you identified?
● Have you thought about value for money and scale of production?
● Have you considered features of other styles and periods?
● Have you tested your design?
● Have you presented your results and evaluation in a suitable manner for your audience?

• D A T A   F I L E •
Food additives

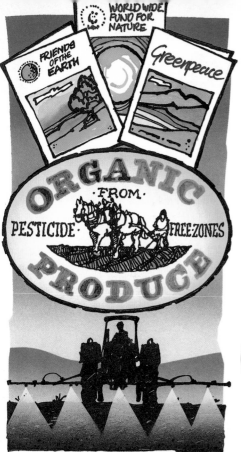

Many people today are concerned about the environment. We hear a lot of talk about 'green' issues. People are concerned about pollution in the rivers, the atmosphere and in the ground. We are all becoming more aware that we need to take more care of our world.

On these two pages are some ideas to do with the environment and conserving precious resources. All this is to do with 'going green'.

GOING *Green*

Many urban areas have derelict sites like this. With a little thought they could be improved for both us and wildlife

Why are the rainforests being destroyed? Who benefits and who suffers? What can be done about it?

We need energy and jobs. We don't need pollution. Coal, oil and gas cannot last forever. What alternatives can you forsee? Are there problems with them too?

Pick one of the ideas on these pages and spend about 10 minutes talking about the idea you have chosen. Share your thoughts and ideas with the rest of the class. Discuss ways in which you can help to change things. What would you like to be able to do? What can you actually do?

MEADOWS

Already 95% of our haymeadows and 80% of the chalk grassland have been lost. Over 50 of our species of wildflowers are threatened with extinction; 19 have already been lost. It is in the old haymeadows where many of our precious wildflowers, and the insects that rely on them, are to be found. In old chalk grassland it is not unusual to find 26 different species in $\frac{1}{16}$ of a square metre of turf. Not so on grassland that has been so-called 'improved' by the addition of fertilizers and manure, here it is mainly grass.

FACTFILE ON

WETLANDS

Over 50% of the marshes and other wetlands have gone, due to widespread pollution, drainage and the building of canals. Have you ever seen a kingfisher? They fish only in clean rivers.

WOODLAND

Forty per cent of our natural woodland has been lost. Pine forests are no replacement for broad-leaved trees, as you would see if you were to take a walk through a pine wood. The forest floor is dark and relatively barren, a far cry from the carpets of bluebells and wood anemones in the ancient broad-leaved woodlands.

WILDLIFE IN THE UK

SEA AND COAST

Two-thirds of the natural coastline of England and Wales has been lost due to pollution, 'improvement' and just overcrowding.

Pick one or two of these places and see if you can find out a bit more about them and the wildlife struggling to survive there. Is there a beach or a wood near you? The other way you could approach this would be to pick a living thing which you think is having a hard time and find out more about the problem, e.g. barn owls, otters, some butterflies, ospreys, or even wild flowers.

GREEN
Campaigners

There are many things in our local communities as well as world-wide which can be made more environmentally friendly or 'greener'. Sometimes we can make an immediate difference ourselves. Sometimes the problems are too big or too complex and we need to persuade others to help. Sometimes it is people's attitudes and values that we don't agree with and this may be the first area that we need to look at.

18,000 dolphins are killed each year by Japanese fishermen, 10,000 a year in Peru, 4,000 a year in Chile to be used as crab bait, 42,000 in Sri Lankan fisheries, 3,000 in American waters in nets set by the Japanese salmon fishermen. Untold thousands die in drift nets in international waters. Public attention has been drawn to the plight of the 120–250,000 dolphins which are killed each year by tuna fishermen who net the dolphins when catching the tuna which are often found swimming beneath them. Pollution is thought to be responsible for causing disease in many more.

The world needs rainforests. They are the lungs of the planet, and have many species of plants and animals found nowhere else which are now threatened with extinction. The forests may have plants that hold the key to the medicines of the future, can we afford to let them be destroyed?

Only 5% of our wildflower meadows that existed up to as late as 1949 are left. Road and motorway verges make up a large area that could help to offset this loss with the right care.

In 1987 the average family of four threw away six trees worth of paper.

The beauty of the coral reefs is threatened not only by pollution but also by the tourist trade. Don't buy marine souvenirs.

Discuss how you feel about the issues on this page. Are there any other green issues that you have views about — whether they are on global or local questions? Do you think there are things which are beyond our control and that we need not concern ourselves with? If you feel you can make a difference, turn to the next page for some project ideas.

MAKING
a difference

First identify a place or an issue that interests you and that you feel strongly about. You could start your design work by planning a survey to see how other people feel about the same thing. Why not use a display of the survey results as part of your campaign?

You should consider the implications of your ideas both on the environment and for people.

Design either a campaign itself or something which could be used as part of a campaign to make a difference in the situation of your choice. For example, you might want to save a village pond from being used as a rubbish dump, or you might want to do something to help to save the rainforests. How will you let people know how you feel? How will you get your message across?

You could design a new T-shirt, tea-towel or set of mugs. You could design a stall at the annual fair to sell your campaign items, or plan to mount a display in a shop window with photographs or a video.

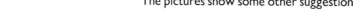

The pictures show some other suggestions.

IS YOUR CAMPAIGN GREEN?

Why not consider campaigning on your own recycled paper? The last thing you want is for people to say that you are wasting paper and valuable trees! It is easy to make and could be used for things such as letters you may need to send, take-away leaflets, information booklets/ commentaries, badges, cards, notepads, etc. Trying to persuade people to use 'tree-free' paper may even become the focus of your campaign. The cost of recycled paper will only come down if more people insist on using it.

NOTE – making recycled paper should only be a part of your project since it does not involve any designing on your part. Your ideas for the campaign and other things that you may design are the most important part.

MAKING RECYCLED PAPER

1 Start with any waste paper you have but avoid glossy papers like magazines. If the paper has print on it your recycled paper will come out grey. Computer paper is best to use; newspaper is worst.

2 Soak the torn up paper in warm water for 10 minutes or more.

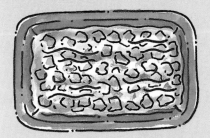

3 Pour some of the mixture into a food blender and whizz until smooth (20–30 seconds). Repeat until all the mixture has been blended.

4 Remove some of the fibres from the slurry onto a screen. The screen can be a metal gauze or a nylon/muslin mesh stretched on a frame such as you might use in screen printing.

5 Place the screen on a cloth and cover it with another.

6 Turn it over and remove the top cloth and screen carefully

7 Replace the cloth on the paper and iron it until the paper begins to dry.

8 Carefully remove the paper and leave it to dry for a day or more in a warm place.

THINK ABOUT

- Experiment with using a little starch or gelatin solution to give your paper a sheen. This will need to be mixed in with the slurry.
- Coloured paper can be made by adding food colouring or you might like to try scenting the paper.

• D A T A   F I L E •

Printing techniques
Storyboard
Advertising
Making a time plan
Presentation techniques

Disused railway lines are often an excellent place for wildlife. We can improve some of them for wildlife and ourselves with thoughtful planning.

What can be done to improve this for everyone and stop it happening again?

WILDLIFE

From this to this!

Trafford Ecological Park, Manchester.

A sterile place for wildlife and not very appealing for us either.

WHERE WE LIVE

We can do so much in our own backyard.

Discuss your local community, home or school and what could be done to improve it for wildlife, and where needs and opportunities for design and technological activities may arise.

Habitat maps & wildlife corridors

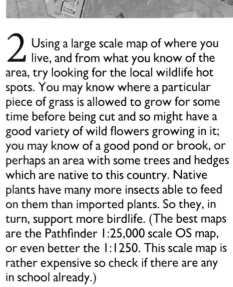

1 Using the aerial photograph shown here, can you identify places that look as if they might be **good** for wildlife. Also have a good look for areas that work like **wildlife corridors** to link up places which encourage wildlife. These corridors are a vital link to encourage wildlife into urban areas. Wildlife corridors may include railway embankments, streams, roadside verges, hedgerows, wooded areas, edges of playing fields, allotments, derelict land, parts of a garden, and so on. You could overlay some clear plastic on this page and mark the areas you identify on this.

Can you see any evidence of how the area used to be – such as hedgerows and roads that no longer exist?

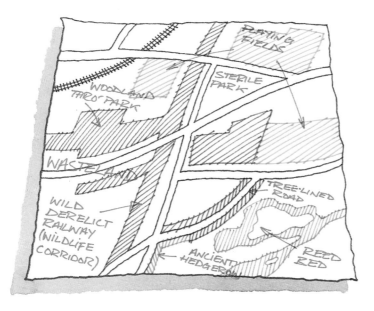

You could try making a map like this one of a local area that you know. Mark on it the good bits for wildlife.

2 Using a large scale map of where you live, and from what you know of the area, try looking for the local wildlife hot spots. You may know where a particular piece of grass is allowed to grow for some time before being cut and so might have a good variety of wild flowers growing in it; you may know of a good pond or brook, or perhaps an area with some trees and hedges which are native to this country. Native plants have many more insects able to feed on them than imported plants. So they, in turn, support more birdlife. (The best maps are the Pathfinder 1:25,000 scale OS map, or even better the 1:1250. This scale map is rather expensive so check if there are any in school already.)

3 You might be able to make a habitat map like the one shown on the left.

4 Research the sites you already know. Perhaps there is a site in or near your school, where there are possibilities for making improvements. You may find a site where a link between two good places needs to be maintained or improved. This could lead to some design ideas. You could make a detailed map of a particular 'wildlife hot spot' and use this as part of a campaign to preserve or enhance the area. On the other hand you might identify a particularly poor area which offers possibilities for improvement. Your research should include a survey of opinions about the site and the improvements you are proposing.

•D A T A   F I L E•

Research techniques
Logos, signs and symbols

Native trees & shrubs

Native trees and shrubs are those that arrived in this country naturally without being introduced either on purpose or accidentally. They are the plants that have been here for a very long time and have become part of our landscape and heritage.

Over a very long time more and more insects have developed to be able to make use of these trees and shrubs. Many of them have caterpillars that eat the leaves. In turn these provides food for many of our birds. If you look at the trees that have been introduced to this country they have much fewer numbers of insect types able to live off them and so are not as good for wildlife, e.g. the insects that feed on the flowering Japanese cherry still live in Japan and cannot survive here.

The alder tree, commonly found near water, is unusual because it is the only broad-leaved tree in this country with cones. Many birds, including siskins, redpolls, reed buntings, tree creepers and woodpeckers feed on the alder seeds found inside the cones.

There are many plants other than trees and shrubs which are enormously valuable to wildlife. Many flowers provide nectar for insects, meadow grasses provide food for the caterpillars of many butterflies and moths but perhaps one of the most useful plants is ivy which has nectar in its flowers in the spring, berries in the autumn and plenty of shelter for nesting birds and overwintering butterflies.

Blue tit

Silver birch

Caterpillar

Squirrel

Dormouse

Hazel

Hazelnuts

NATIVE					
Tree or Shrub	Number of insect species	Tree or Shrub	Number of insect species	Tree or Shrub	Number of insect species
Oak	284	Hazel	73	Spruce	37
Willow	266	Beech	64	Larch	17
Birch	229	Ash	41	Fir	16
Hawthorn	149	Lime	31	Sycamore	15
Blackthorn	109	Rowan	28	Sweet chestnut	5
Poplar	97	Hornbeam	28	Horse chestnut	4
Apple	93	Field Maple	26		
Pine	91	Holly	7		
Alder	90	Yew	1		
Elm	82				

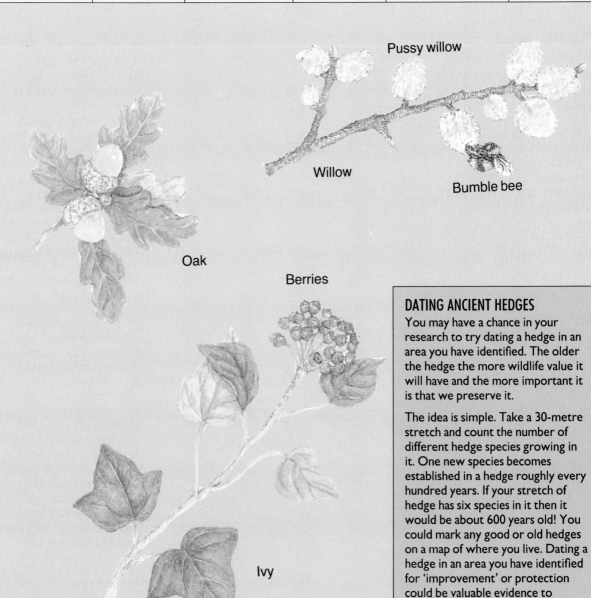

Pussy willow

Willow

Bumble bee

Oak

Berries

Ivy

DATING ANCIENT HEDGES

You may have a chance in your research to try dating a hedge in an area you have identified. The older the hedge the more wildlife value it will have and the more important it is that we preserve it.

The idea is simple. Take a 30-metre stretch and count the number of different hedge species growing in it. One new species becomes established in a hedge roughly every hundred years. If your stretch of hedge has six species in it then it would be about 600 years old! You could mark any good or old hedges on a map of where you live. Dating a hedge in an area you have identified for 'improvement' or protection could be valuable evidence to support your design ideas.

THINK **BIG**

There are many opportunities to encourage and enjoy wildlife in and around where we all live. Having taken a good look at your local area to see if there are things which would improve things for wildlife, you now need to make a decision about what you are going to design. Just think, if everyone did just a little, what it would do to help across the country.

Part of changing the whole scene relies on people seeing the good that is done and being able to enjoy the wildlife. We need the quiet spots for breeding birds and animals but we also need the bird hides, walk-ways across the marshes and ponds and information boards so that we can enjoy the wildlife.

I In your 'thinking big' activity you could consider redesigning a whole area. You need to research the scheme first by seeing if there is something similar in your neighbourhood. If so, there may be a model of it at the site office, or perhaps on display in the library or council offices. If not, your local reference librarian can find you a leisure directory that lists countryside parks. Their entries and advertisements should give you some ideas.

You might include a cost schedule, graphic representations of how you would like the scheme to look, or even a model. Think about how you would convince others that it is a good idea, drafting out a management plan of how to look after it in future. How will you tell people in the community about it? How will you inform visitors about the special features of the site? Is there scope for a park and ride scheme for visitors?

Don't forget to record the opinions of others about the whole idea at various stages in your folio.

THINK SMALL

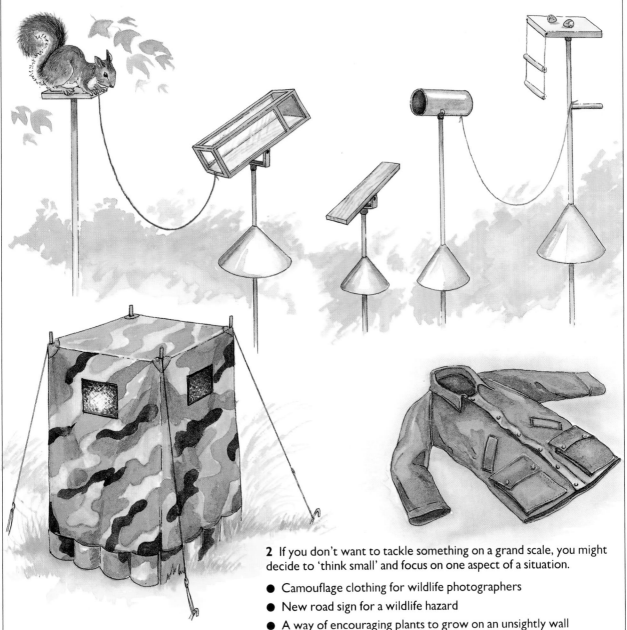

2 If you don't want to tackle something on a grand scale, you might decide to 'think small' and focus on one aspect of a situation.

- Camouflage clothing for wildlife photographers
- New road sign for a wildlife hazard
- A way of encouraging plants to grow on an unsightly wall
- Design for a butterfly garden
- Sound and waterproofed case for that special camera shot
- Mini-enterprise scheme for producing wildflower seeds
- Underwater viewer for pond life
- Small mammal viewing hide
- Portable hide for wildlife watching
- Assault course for the local squirrels before they get to the food

• D A T A   F I L E •

Ideas for modelling
Flowcharts
Modelling
Joining

GROWING *Green*

Growing your own vegetables and fruit can be a green thing to do but it may not be. Which of the following things do you think are environmentally friendly and which are not? Growing for profit, growing to save money, spraying to kill pests, using chemical fertilisers, using machines to help with jobs like digging the soil, using hand tools, encouraging helpful insects to remove pests, using manure as a fertiliser, growing more in the space available, removing trees and hedges to make room for more crops?

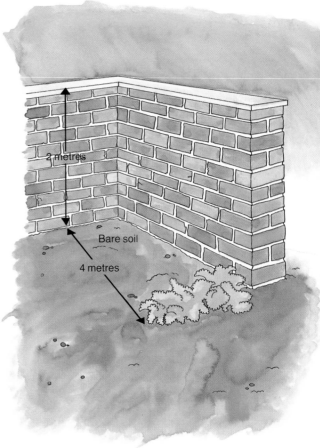

SAVING MONEY

One of the reasons why people often grow their own is the hope of saving money. However, it is not always easy to see how much money is being saved or even if it is really cheaper than buying the food from the shops. One good way of looking at the situation is to use a spreadsheet on a computer.

To see how it works try entering the data in the table on a spreadsheet. You can add more data of your own or change the numbers given in the table if you think they are not realistic. Once you have set up the spreadsheet, try altering some costs to see the effect it has on the balance between profit and loss, e.g. try including the cost of Gro-bags for tomatoes.

Table of data on fruit and vegetables

Vegetable	Seed cost £	Fertiliser cost (£4.30 for 25 kg) £	Gro-bags (@ £2 each) £	Sundry items e.g. canes £	Est. yield per plant (lbs)	shop price per lb £
Runner beans	0.99	0 (use manure)		2	2	0.95
Peas	0.99	0 (use manure)			0.1	0.65 (frozen)
Carrots	0.59	1			0.4	0.32
Lettuce	0.59	1			0.5	0.29 each
Tomatoes	0.69	1	6		8	0.69
Cabbage	1.25	1			4	0.25
Sprouts	1.30	1			4	0.62

DIY Spreadsheet

	A	B	C	D	E	F	G	H	I	J	K	L
1		Example of how to start a spreadsheet on the cost of growing your own										
2												
3	Vegetable	Seed cost	Fertiliser cost	Gro-bags	Sundry items	Total growing cost	Number of plants	Expected yield per	Total	Shop Price	Crop Value	Cost Saving
4		(£.p)	(£4.30/25 kg)	(£2 each)	canes etc.			plant (lbs)	Yield (lbs)	(£/lb)	(£.p)	(£.p)
5												
6	Tomatoes	0.69	1.00			1.69	9.00	8.00	72.00	0.69	49.68	47.99
7	Carrots	0.59	1.00			1.59	25.00	0.40	10.00	0.32	3.20	1.61
8	etc.											
9												
10	Calculations that are needed:–					Sum of B to E			G × H	J × I	K − F	

Making Space for growing green

1 Can you design a plot so that the crops don't get trampled as you weed the area and you don't get muddy getting to your crop. The designs should be costed out.

2 Could you start a mini-enterprise to raise money for school or another organisation, perhaps involving the design of hydroponics units to produce cress, herbs or barley? This system uses no soil, only water and plant fertiliser.

3 How would you devise a system for growing blue-green algae so that it can be added to the soil to provide natural fertiliser? These algae trap nitrogen from the air and turn it into nitrates which plants use to help them grow. Algae are easy to grow as they only need water, air and a few mineral salts.

4 There are ways of growing vegetables which avoid the use of pesticides as far as possible. You might consider using plants which attract helpful insects or which repel pests. You could design something which traps pests or prevents them from entering the plot at all. (Slugs might not crawl over very rough/sharp surfaces; shielding carrot plants with natural or artificial barriers prevents the carrot fly from seeing them as it flies by; slugs are attracted to yeasty/alcoholic smells as in left-over beer.)

5 Fruit and vegetables can be grown in a variety of places:

● window box
● flat roof garden
● allotment
● small urban garden
● greenhouse.

You could select one of these or a similar situation and design a way of growing vegetables which makes the very best use of the available growing space.

You could choose to focus upon the area shown opposite here as a starting point.

6 Consider how best to grow runner beans, strawberries, tomatoes and blackberries in this corner to get the best possible yield from this space. You might consider ways of growing plants up the wall or even trailing down the wall, mini-greenhouses, wire/cane/string structures, netting structures which use the space between the walls etc.

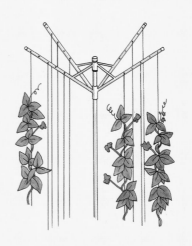

• D A T A   F I L E •

Structures
Joining
Information systems

Getting
THE BEST
from
THE BEST!

Home-grown fruits and vegetables can be more colourful and tasty than those bought in supermarkets. Often there are days or weeks between the time they are picked and the time they are displayed for sale. Home-grown produce is also better for us because it can be grown free from chemical pesticides (sprays) and can be harvested and used speedily. Because of this it is also likely to be better nutritionally, though public demand for healthier food has resulted in more shops offering organically grown fruit and vegetables for sale, that is, grown without chemical fertilisers and pesticides.

There is little point in growing or buying organic food for the family if it is not used properly in the kitchen. It is vital to store, handle, prepare and cook the food properly in order to retain its nutritional value.

Draw up a checklist of points to follow when using fresh fruits and vegetables in cooking.

Top: braised red cabbage; bottom left: corn with cheese sauce; bottom right: broccoli casserole.

In this section we are looking at getting the best value from the best food.

1 Start by choosing a recipe for a simple dish made mainly from vegetables. Then, analyse its nutritional content. Using guidelines for a recommended healthy diet, how acceptable would this dish be as part of that diet?

Redesign the dish to improve it nutritionally and suggest a category of person it would be suitable for, e.g. an athlete, someone recovering from a heart attack. Show how it is more nutritionally sound in a table comparing the food value originally with your improvements.

2 Celebrate the best of your natural harvest by designing your own two-course meal on a theme, using organically grown fruits and vegetables easily available for the time of the year. State what accompaniments you would serve with the meal.

Design a table plan, menu and display which is attractive and yet gives the clear message that this is the best food you can get. (Be careful not to add ingredients that put the chemicals back in!)

Using the theme you could then design items for serving it, including napkins, napkin holders, tablecloths, dishes, plates, tureens, salt and pepper pots or a flower display.

3 You may want to tell your friends and their parents about your ideas for organic produce by designing an information booklet, recipe cards or a video.

• D A T A   F I L E •
Special diets

SAVING IT

We tend to harvest more food than we can eat immediately so it would be useful to suggest methods of preserving fruit and vegetables for use later on.

Look at the suitability of freezing fruit or vegetables whole or as a made dish; of storing them as preserves such as pickles and chutney, drying, etc.

The nutritional value of these items may not be ideal but it prevents wastage and they will be much cheaper to make than buy. You could check this out at your local supermarket.

Ask at the supermarket if they have requests for organic vegetables, or if they already sell them.

Design a stand for promoting organic vegetables at your local supermarket where you could give customers leaflets at the same time as offering them tasters.

Decide where to place the stand and what it should look like to attract the public.

Produce an attractive leaflet promoting organic gardening and giving recipe suggestions.

Suggest a few dishes for tasters to demonstrate the versatility of both fruits and vegetables.

Perhaps recipe cards of these dishes could be given as promotional material.

There is a category of people who rely solely on vegetables as the mainstay of their diet: vegetarians – many of whom do not eat animal products or by-products. There are a variety of reasons for this:

- religion
- health
- moral beliefs
- personal preference.

A religious ceremony in India

Find out as much detail as possible about a religion that follows a vegetarian diet and the guidelines that it suggests should be observed.

- What types of foods/dishes are generally served?
- What is the staple food eaten?
- How are the dishes made colourful?
- What cooking methods are used?
- Why is such a variety of herbs and spices used?

Suggest a typical meal for a family of that religion and analyse its nutritional content.

What are the dishes eaten by the family during their religious festivals?

How easy is it to buy the necessary ingredients for such food in your community?

. D A T A   F I L E .

Nutritional guidelines
Research techniques

Versatile vegetables

If you could take your investigations to the country of origin of vegetarian dishes, you would discover other reasons why this type of food is traditionally served:

- climatic conditions
- type of agricultural equipment used
- type of soil or land
- lifestyle, for example, nomadic

In most cases people grow foods that are easiest to produce and yield the largest crops. By comparison to cattle rearing, growing crops is a much more economical use of land.

Storing food is also a major concern, especially in hot countries, and may well be the reason why pulse vegetables are so popular – they are easily stored once harvested. If kept dry the storage life of most pulses is long – approximately a year in ideal conditions.

Pulse vegetables have become more popular in recent years as we have become more concerned with the content of our diets. Not only can they be used as a cheaper substitute for meat with their high protein and low fat content but they are high in dietary fibre and are a valuable source of vitamins and minerals.

Visit your local supermarket or health food store and list the pulses on sale. You could, at the same time, look at the variety of different rices on the shelves.

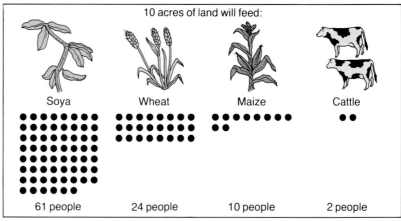

10 acres of land will feed:

Soya	Wheat	Maize	Cattle
61 people	24 people	10 people	2 people

The pulses are (from bottom left to right): black-eyed beans; mung beans; chickpeas; pinto beans; red kidney beans; sunflower seeds; black kidney beans; red lentils; marrow fat peas; yellow split peas; kibbled wheat; hazelnuts; aduki beans; butter beans; green split peas; garlic; haricot beans; pine kernels; wheat grain; sesame seeds; maize; pumpkin seeds; organic short grain rice; pecan nuts; flagelot beans; organic rice flakes; wheatgerm. The herbs are thyme and dill.

CHICK PEA AND CAULIFLOWER CURRY

2 tablespoons oil
2 cloves garlic, crushed
1–2 green chillies, seeded
 and sliced
2.5 cm (1 inch) piece fresh
 root ginger, grated
1 large onion, chopped
1 teaspoon each turmeric,
 paprika, ground
 coriander, and
 fenugreek seeds
2 teaspoons ground cumin
1/4 teaspoon cinnamon
1 tablespoon tomato purée

1 litre (1¾ pints) vegetable
 stock
1 tablespoon lemon juice
250 g (8 oz) small
 potatoes, halved
1 small cauliflower,
 broken into florets
250 g (8 oz) chick peas,
 cooked
3 tablespoons natural
 yogurt
2 tablespoons desiccated
 coconut
salt and pepper to taste

1. Heat the oil in a pan, add the garlic, chillies, ginger and onion and fry for about 5 minutes. Add the spices and fry for 1–2 minutes, then add the tomato purée, stock, lemon juice, and salt and pepper and bring to the boil.
2. Add the potatoes, cover and cook for 5 minutes. Add the cauliflower and chick peas, cover and simmer for 15 minutes or until the potatoes are tender.
3. Add yogurt, top with coconut and serve with rice.

Serves 4
Preparation time:
20 minutes, plus
cooking chick pea
Cooking time:
25–30 minutes
Freezing:
Recommended

VEGETABLE AND BEAN COUS COUS

500 g (1 lb) cous cous
2 tablespoons olive oil
25 g (1 oz) butter
1 large onion, sliced
1 clove garlic, crushed
2 carrots, sliced
250 g (8 oz) parsnips,
 diced
1 teaspoon each turmeric
 and ground coriander
125 g (4 oz) white beans,
 cooked

125 g (4 oz) button
 mushrooms
175 g (6 oz) French beans,
 halved
4 tomatoes, skinned and
 quartered
300 ml (½ pint) each
 vegetable stock and dry
 cider
6 canned artichoke hearts,
 halved
salt and pepper to taste

Serves 4–6
Preparation time:
30 minutes, plus
cooking beans
Cooking time:
20 minutes
Freezing:
Not recommended

1. Prepare the cous cous according to packet instructions if easy-cook, or as for Cous Cous with Spiced Lamb (page 40).
2. Heat the oil and butter in a pan, add the onion, garlic, carrot and parsnip and fry gently for 10 minutes, or until softened. Sprinkle in the spices and cook for 1 minute.
3. Add the remaining ingredients, except the cous cous, and bring to the boil.
4. Put the cous cous into a steamer that fits on top of the saucepan, cover and simmer for about 20 minutes.
5. Serve the cous cous topped with the vegetables.

1 Find out how to cook pulses successfully and look for an interesting recipe using a pulse vegetable that you have never tasted. Once you have made the dish you could have a food tasting panel to find out what other people think of it.

2 Having now experienced the preparation and cooking of pulses you should know some of the important points to remember when using these in cooking.

To show how versatile these vegetables are, design your own recipe for a side dish mainly using pulses which would be suitable for serving with a salad. Think how you could introduce interesting colours and textures and how to add to the nutritional value of that meal.

• D A T A   F I L E •

Research techniques
Presenting information

ALTERNATIVE

ost people are aware that the world's energy resources – based on fossil fuels of coal, oil and gas – are running out. If we carry on using the fuels at the present rate, using the reserves that we know exist, then oil is due to run out by the year 2030, gas by 2045 and coal by 2240. Of course we may need to use more fuel in the future as the population grows!

We all know that burning these fuels causes pollution of various kinds and so there is a real need to explore alternative ways of making energy.

We have some wind turbines already, and now a power station using biogas from chicken droppings is to be built. It is estimated that the energy from this power station will be enough to serve 10,000 homes.

The pie chart shows the proportion of Britain's energy produced from various sources in 1986.

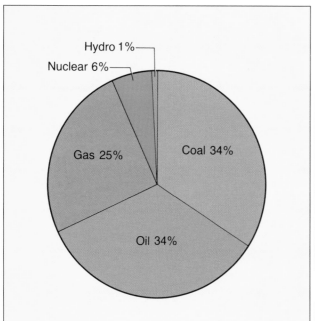

- Hydro 1%
- Nuclear 6%
- Gas 25%
- Coal 34%
- Oil 34%

There are environmental problems linked to most methods of producing energy, especially for use on a national scale.

Try to complete a table to show the advantages and disadvantages of the various energy sources. You might also like to consider if any of the waste products from generating energy can be used to help in some way, e.g. waste heat.

Wood chips being poured into a biogas generator, microbes rot the waste to make the gas. How can the gas be used to make electricity?

As the tide rises water is allowed into the river estuary. As the tide falls the water flows out through the turbines to make electricity.

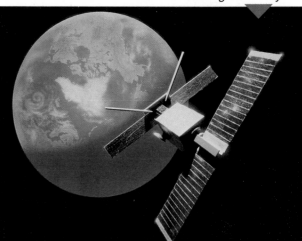

Solar cells on a satellite used for making electricity.

ENERGY

Some of the alternative ways of producing energy which may become more attractive in the future are:

- using the wind
- using biogas (methane)
- using sunlight
- using tidal power

These sources are renewable, unlike the fossil fuels, which take millions of years to be formed below the earth.

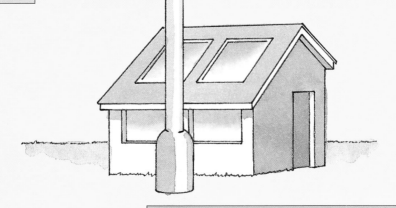

Solar panels used for heating water in London ▲

Yet, not even these systems are perfect. What do you think about them? Did you know, for instance, that biogas generators produce methane which is one of the 'greenhouse' gases? Of course it is normally burned off but this produces carbon dioxide which is also a greenhouse gas. Power stations have been producing carbon dioxide for years.

What about the wind turbines that would need to be built in banks across the sky line – perhaps along those very pieces of coastline that are so pretty. What happens when the wind is not blowing hard enough to make much electricity?

The next two sections look in more detail at wind power and solar energy.

If you connect a battery to a small motor with two wires then the motor will turn. In this case electrical energy has been changed into movement or kinetic energy. But did you know that if you attach the motor to a bulb in a simple circuit and turn the motor the bulb will light up? Why not try it for yourself? In this case movement energy is changed into light energy.

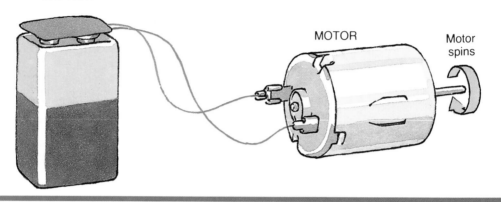

BATTERY

MOTOR

Motor spins

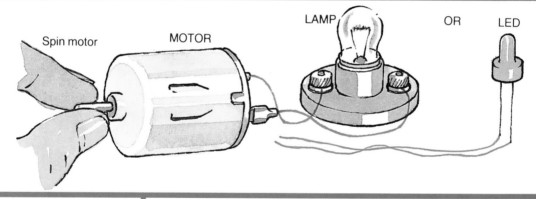

Spin motor

MOTOR

LAMP

OR

LED

You can measure the amount of electricity produced (voltage) by attaching the motor to a voltmeter and turning the spindle of the motor.

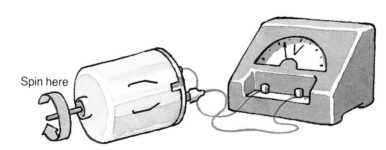

Spin here

This idea is the principle by which bicycle dynamos work and also the giant wind turbines which are appearing in the Scottish Highlands.

• D A T A   F I L E •

Fair testing
Structures
Movement
Electrical circuits

POWER

You could try to design a wind turbine for yourself.

You may need to involve some gearing so that a slow speed of movement of the propeller will result in a fast speed of movement of the motor spindle.

What about the design of the propeller? Can you try to improve this? You could start by looking at pictures of propellers that exist now, both modern ones and traditional designs. Why not have a go at designing a testing rig for your propeller designs so that you can see which is really the best?

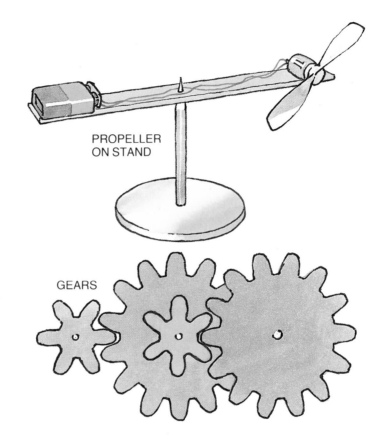

PROPELLER
ON STAND

GEARS

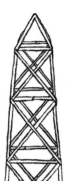

WIND
TURBINE

What about the structure of the tower that will hold the propeller and the dynamo (motor)? You could practise making a good structure by using paper art straws and a good glue, perhaps with card strips to help. Or what about using dry, uncooked spaghetti and a strong glue? (Do not use superglue.)

All your design work and the results of any tests you may run should be recorded in your folio. If you have looked at designs from the past, or from other countries, then make a note of your thoughts about them too.

You need to think about what material you are going to make your final model out of and try modelling with that material.

Solar energy is used occasionally in this country, but more often abroad, to make electricity for heating, cooking and lighting, etc. Solar panels are sometimes used to heat water but in this section we will try designing and using solar cells which are good at changing light energy into electricity. If you need more power than one solar cell can produce then you need to link a number of cells together to form an array. They need to be wired up in series to give a higher voltage and in parallel to give more current if you want to use a larger motor than the special one designed for use with solar cells (see Datafile on solar panels).

You need to decide on a context for your project. Here are some ideas:

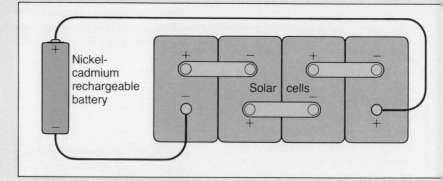

1 You could use solar panels to provide lighting for homes in Third World countries without electricity. The light energy needs to be stored in a battery for use at night. This could involve making a model of the house you are hoping to light.

2 You could design the prototype for a solar powered warning buoy for shipping in tropical waters. The solar cells could be used to charge up rechargeable batteries which would then be used only at night (and perhaps also in fog). You would need some simple systems electronics to sort out the switching for this which could be wired to be outside the water tank or sink. In the real thing the electronics could be made small enough to go on the buoy.

To get a flashing bulb you have a number of options to explore:

You can get special motors that work well with solar panels which can be used to turn a film canister. The canister can be placed over the bulb and modified to shield the bulb for part of the time, while a hole cut in the canister gives the warning light that the ships need.

Another way is to use the pulse generator on MFA, or other systems electronics boards, to send pulses to the bulb to make it flash. Or you could try an electro-mechanical mechanism, see pictures.

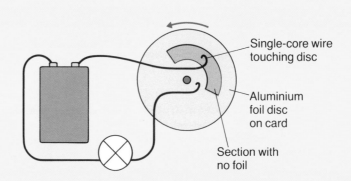

Single-core wire touching disc

Aluminium foil disc on card

Section with no foil

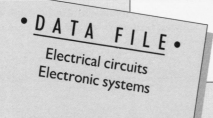

• D A T A   F I L E •
Electrical circuits
Electronic systems

POWER

3 Why not consider a solar powered system for running your tape recorder at home, or perhaps a train set or doll's house?

Another idea is to design a system for lifting water from wells in hot countries using the plentiful sunlight energy. You could try using a windscreen washer pump with the solar panels for this. A pump of this sort will run on a range of voltages from 4 to 12 volts but it will need quite a bit of current. You would need a lot of solar cells arranged in series and in parallel to run the motor direct but why not assume for your project that the pump is only used at dusk when the batteries are fully charged? After all it would be cooler for the people carrying the water back to the villages at that time than in the middle of the day. The water could be collected in earthenware pots which leak water very slowly. This should have the effect of keeping the water cool for drinking. Can you find out why?

It is also possible to buy leds that flash.

You would need to think about the fact that a flashing led needs 4.75 volts to 7 volts to work properly. One typical battery gives 1.5 volts so your solar panels would need to charge up 3 to 4 batteries. (This type of led does not need a protective resistor to limit the current.) Also remember that the light from a led is given out in a particular direction, not like a light bulb. Ships would be able to see it only if they were in the right place which isn't really a good idea. You could get round this by using more leds. They might flash at different times of course but you can think of something for that problem!

You need to consider, among other things, the stability of the buoy since rough seas are very common.

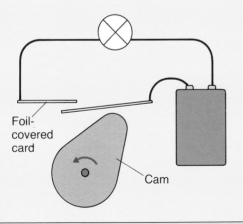

Foil-covered card

Cam

Finally after all the talk recently about 'green' cars, why not have a go at designing your very own solar powered car? The solar panels would need to be used to charge up a battery or two and the car run from these. Again running the car in the sunlight without a battery backup would require a lot of solar cells.

Pollution

In these sections we look at pollution in our local community. In particular we focus on air, water and noise pollution.

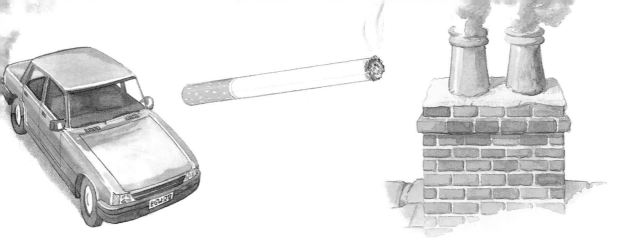

Detectives

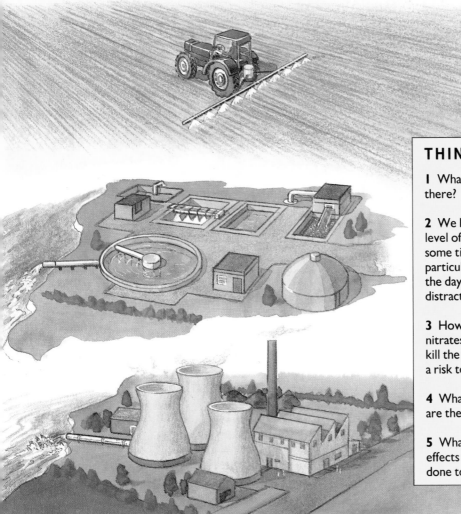

THINK ABOUT

1 What types of air pollution are there?

2 We have learned to live with some level of noise pollution. There are some times when we find noise particularly annoying. What times in the day would or do you find noise distracting?

3 How is it that fertilisers such as nitrates, which help crops grow, can kill the fish in our rivers and may pose a risk to human health?

4 What is a smokeless zone and why are there such things?

5 What causes acid rain, what are its effects on wildlife and what can be done to prevent it?

There are many different types of air pollution. We hear about acid rain, about carbon monoxide from car exhausts, about the 'greenhouse gases' like carbon dioxide and methane, but there is another pollutant which blackens our buildings and trees. It is made up mainly of soot and dirt as tiny particles which are carried in the air and which then settle out to form a layer of grime over everything. It comes from cars, factories, fires at home and of course from dusty places like roads and building sites.

Air

As a pollution detective can you design something to measure the amount of dirt falling out of our skies over a period of a week or two?

Your design needs to be rain-proof and animal-proof, and to give a measure of the amount of pollution, perhaps visually or perhaps measured by some other means, e.g. electronically. It also needs to be something that you can actually make and test.

You need to think about whether to base it on the idea that pollution settles like dust from the air, or whether to try to draw the air through a filter by some sort of suction mechanism? You will need to test the air over a fairly long period of time in order to see a result.

British Gas makes a meter that could be used to measure the amount of air passed through something over long periods of time.

Pollution

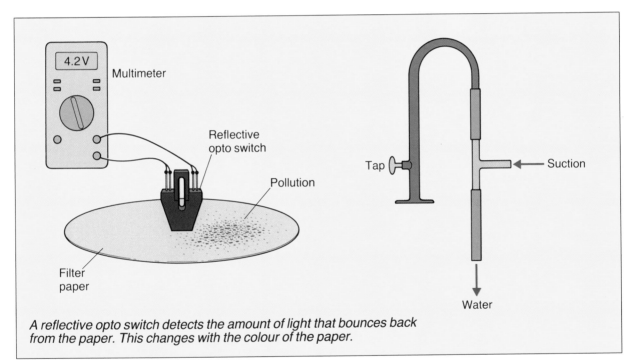

A reflective opto switch detects the amount of light that bounces back from the paper. This changes with the colour of the paper.

Having tried out and tested your design you will need to think about whether improvements can be made.

Can you use your design to do some detective work in different places to see if the pollution levels are better or worse? For instance, is the pollution worse in the city or the countryside? Is it worse near roads? Is it the same all year round?

• D A T A   F I L E •

Fair testing
Materials
Evaluating

In this section we look at designing ways to reduce noise. Noise pollution comes from many things in the world around us. Many of us might prefer to live with less noise if we had a choice. It is not until we go to a really quiet place that we notice the sounds we live with each day: traffic, aeroplanes, bells, crowds, road machinery, building sites, or even noise at home. Perhaps there is someone where you live who plays loud music? Many everyday things like cars and washing machines are quieter than they used to be but they can still be a nuisance.

You could survey opinions at home or in your neighbourhood about noises that annoy people and how noise affects their lives. What about noise in times gone by? Did they have noise pollution then or is it only a modern problem?

Noise

You need to identify some everyday object that causes a nuisance. You might choose a washing machine as an example. Then design the best possible sound-proofing system for it.

One solution might be to surround the machine with something which deadens the noise. The diagram shows how a test rig can be set up so that you can try different types of sound-proofing materials.

But first you need a noise for the tests. Your teacher may be able to provide you with a sound generator, or you could tape a real washing machine spinning and rewind it for each test.

You also need an oscilloscope to measure the sound. You could cut out a piece of clear plastic to cover the screen of the oscilloscope and mark the results of your tests on it.

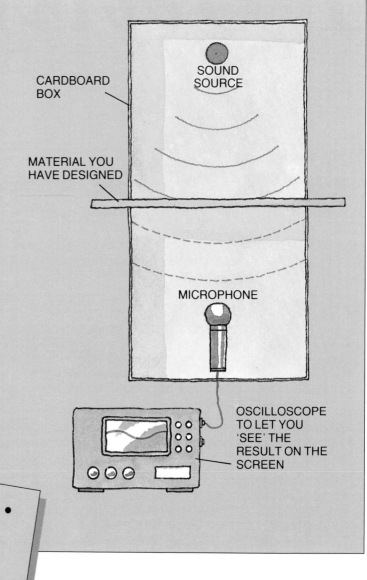

CARDBOARD BOX

SOUND SOURCE

MATERIAL YOU HAVE DESIGNED

MICROPHONE

OSCILLOSCOPE TO LET YOU 'SEE' THE RESULT ON THE SCREEN

• D A T A   F I L E •
Electronic systems
Evaluating

Pollution

You should try different types of sound-proofing materials, in different thicknesses, with different surfaces. Think about joining them together in layers – some will join together better than others. Some cost more than others. Some are waterproof, some strong, some flexible. Why not make a database of your findings so that you, or other people, can use the information again?

The list below gives you some ideas. Be sure to keep notes of everything in your folio.

When you have designed what you think is the best solution you should make a model to show how it works. If you have chosen to sound-proof a washing machine you could use a tape recording of a really noisy washing machine inside your model.

carpet

card

plastic

rubber

polystyrene

corrugated card

corriflute plastic

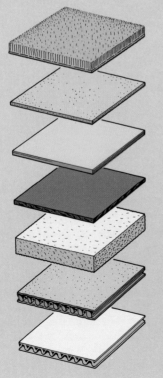

metal sheet

paper

wood

fabric

styrofoam blocks

combination of materials

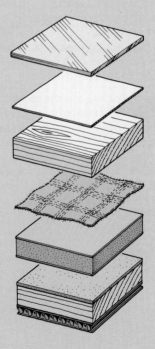

Your local water authority is concerned about the pollution of rivers and canals and would like to commission a study into the problem. They have approached your design team to ask you to try to suggest some workable solutions.

Their main concern is pollution by fertilisers. The over-use of fertilisers on fields causes the chemicals in them to be washed by the rain into the rivers. In Britain some 30% of the nitrates applied to crops may be lost.

You can see a similar thing in gardens when some ponds go green like pea soup in the summer.

On the Norfolk Broads, the waterways are very badly polluted this way because the extra nitrates cause algae to grow too fast. Normally there are little creatures called daphnia in the water which eat the algae and keep the situation under control. The trouble is that the daphnia can't keep up with all the algae because they themselves are a delicacy for the fish to eat. If only there was a way of protecting the daphnia from the fish the problem would be solved.

You might think that the answer is to reduce the amount of nitrate fertiliser used. However, even if farmers used much less fertiliser from now on there are so many nutrients locked up in the mud on the bottom of the waterways that the situation would take years before it improved.

Water

You can test to see how much nitrate there is in water very easily. There are little test strips called 'Snappy Sap Tests' that were designed for farmers to test the sap of their crops. If they are over-using nitrates, then too much appears in the sap of plants. You could use these test strips to test tap water, soil water, the sap of vegetables you buy in the shops, or the water from a garden pond, river or canal. You need only to dip the end of the strip in the water or sap and wait for 60 seconds before checking the colour produced against a given scale.

• D A T A F I L E •

Fair testing
Structures
Materials

The daphnia need places to hide from the fish. There are many possible ways of helping them.

Pollution

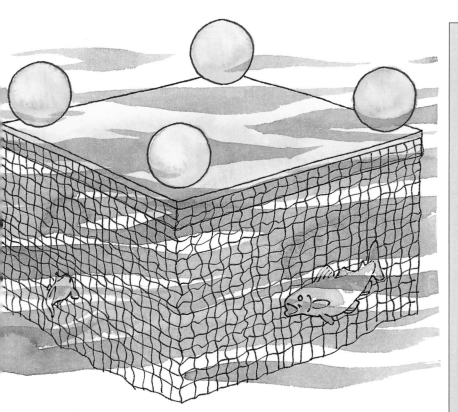

You don't need to prevent all the daphnia from being eaten by fish as they do breed very quickly.

You could decide to design something for a garden pond, slow flowing river or canal. You need to consider the scale of the system, whether it would stay in place all the time, whether it would get in the way of boats or people fishing, how much it would cost and if it needs replacing or maintenance. Would the material rot quickly in water, would it float or sink, would it be something which people would want to buy?

FACT FILE ON DAPHNIA

1 They are small creatures (0.5–3 mm) related to shrimps (crustacea) and can be seen in their hundreds in a jar of pond water in the summer.

2 They feed by filtering the water to trap the tiny algae.

3 They have an eye spot and are attracted to light.

4 They swim in a hopping type of movement. They are not good swimmers and so cannot live in fast flowing rivers.

5 They multiply very quickly in the warm weather. If you look at an adult daphnia under a microscope you can often see the young ones inside a protective pouch.

6 Aquarium shops often sell daphnia in polythene bags as live fish food.

A BULB
IN A BOX
is worth two in the ground

Frinton Ferries are promoting springtime sailings to Holland. As part of the promotion, each passenger will receive an individually packaged specially selected tulip bulb, complete with growing instructions.

The packaging firm which Frinton Ferries approached have suggested the box shown. Frinton Ferries do not think this is suitable and have decided to design and make their own packaging.

This is the box produced by the packaging firm. Make this box using the dimensions given from a piece of card. This could be 'found' materials such as an old cereal packet.

———— cut   – – – – – fold

• D A T A   F I L E •
Nets/developments
Evaluating

Now consider what Frinton Ferries really need.

A team from Frinton Ferries have brainstormed ideas for their promotional box.

WHAT'S IN THE BOX?

INFORMATION ON BOX?

DOES IT NEED TO OPEN?

WHAT IS BEING PROMOTED?

COLOUR?

SHAPE?

STRENGTH?

PROMOTIONAL BOX

NEED TO SEE OBJECT IN BOX?

LOGO?

CONSTRUCTION METHODS?

MATERIAL?

COST?

STACKABILITY?

CONTAINER?

PACKAGING?

BAG?

BOX?

WRAPPING?

ADVERTISING?

POSTER?

POP-UP CARD?

What size is a tulip bulb?
What instructions are needed for successful growing?
How important is colour?
Do the boxes need to be stacked?

These are only some of the questions asked. In your team decide how you would develop the promotion using the brainstorm.

CREATING NEW DESIGNS

O ne very useful way to create exciting new designs is shown here. You can use this approach to help in your design work in other projects too.

It will help you to produce ideas for surface designs or patterns and for the shape or form of things.

You could try the ideas given here or decide on the starting point for yourself.

The idea can be explained in stages although in practice you will find you won't work strictly like this.

STARTING POINTS

Set up some visually interesting starting points which allow you to explore the qualities of what you see. This could be done on a theme, such as falling water, sport, autumn, holidays, etc. You could use something set up by your teacher or you may be asked to create your own starting point. For Frinton Ferries it seems sensible to start by exploring the qualities of falling or gently moving water or perhaps tulips since the ferry is taking people to Holland. Remember that the box is a freebie and is to contain one or perhaps more bulbs. The idea is to please people travelling with the ferry company to make them remember the crossing in a way which might encourage them to use it again or to tell their friends about it.

Water occurs in various states . . . static, running, falling, etc

KEYWORDS

Reflecting
Shimmering
Dribbling

Splashing
Distorting
Bubbling
Crashing

EXPLORING VISUAL QUALITIES

Make some drawings of what you see in your starting point. Focus on those parts that you find visually interesting. Don't think about the end product at this stage, just draw freely what you see. You might want to make a number of drawings of different aspects, or you might try using different materials and media, e.g. colour, torn paper or charcoal.

•DATA FILE•

Sketching
Artists materials

DEVELOPING YOUR ◊ IDEAS

Have a look at what you have produced and pick those parts that you feel have worked well and are interesting. These could then be developed to produce something close to a design you might use. Remember, that in this case, you might be looking for a design for the card or perhaps a new shape for the box or perhaps both of these things. Your ideas may even lend themselves to new ways of doing the lettering. At some stage you will need to decide what words should appear on the box and how these could best be blended in with the design.

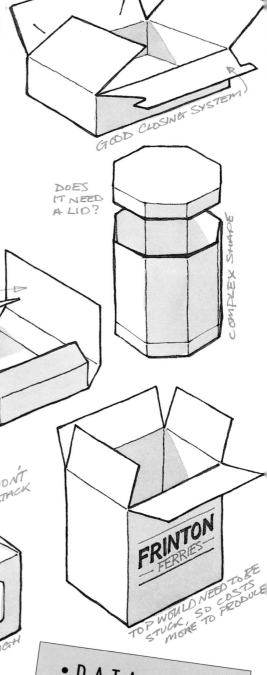

GOOD CLOSING SYSTEM

DOES IT NEED A LID?

COMPLEX SHAPE

shape

THIS SHAPE MAY PACK WELL

INSTRUCTIONS ON INSIDE OF LID

BULB MOTIF

THIS WON'T STACK

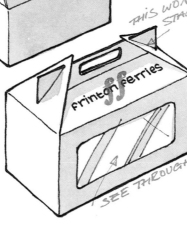

frinton ferries ff

SEE THROUGH

FRINTON FERRIES

TOP WOULD NEED TO BE STUCK, SO COSTS MORE TO PRODUCE

• D A T A   F I L E •
Presentation techniques
Printing techniques

surface designs

FINISHED PRODUCT

F f

FRINTON
FERRIES

Frinton
Ferries

frinton *ff* ferries

FRINTON
— FERRIES —

Enjoy your trip

logos

FINAL DESIGN

You might now have developed a number of useful ideas or you may have one that you are pleased with. If a number of ideas have come out then think about using the good points from the different designs to produce something even better. Try out your final design by making the box. The experience of making the box may well show up problems that you had not spotted and so be prepared to rethink your ideas at all stages.

83

What do **you** mean by a home?

Home is not just the place where we live. Home should be where we feel we belong.

People in different parts of the world, and in different parts of this country, live in different types of accommodation. Their needs are not all the same. Look at the different types of dwellings shown on these pages.

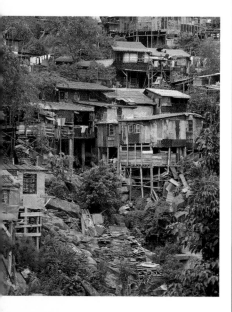

the
HOME

The pupils at your school probably come from a wide area around the school, an area containing a wide range of housing. What are the different types of accommodation near you?

Different houses and homes can tell you something about:

- the people who built them
- the needs of people who live in them
- the surrounding environment.

Look at the pictures on these two pages. What thoughts come to your mind as you look at the different types of accommodation?

Homes are built for a variety of reasons:

● for shelter
● for protection
● to form a community.

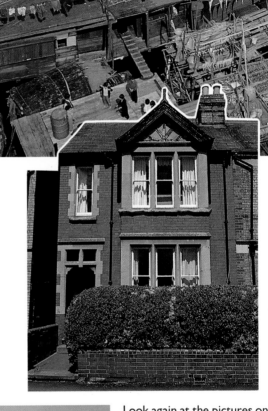

Look again at the pictures on these two pages. Choose one of the examples and discuss:

● the needs of the builder
● the needs of the owner or occupier
● the materials it is made from
● whether the dwelling is permanent
● the environment in which it is found
● the weather conditions it has to face.

Make notes during your discussion. They may help you with projects later.

The rooms where you live

Different rooms have different uses, and sometimes the same room has different uses at different times.

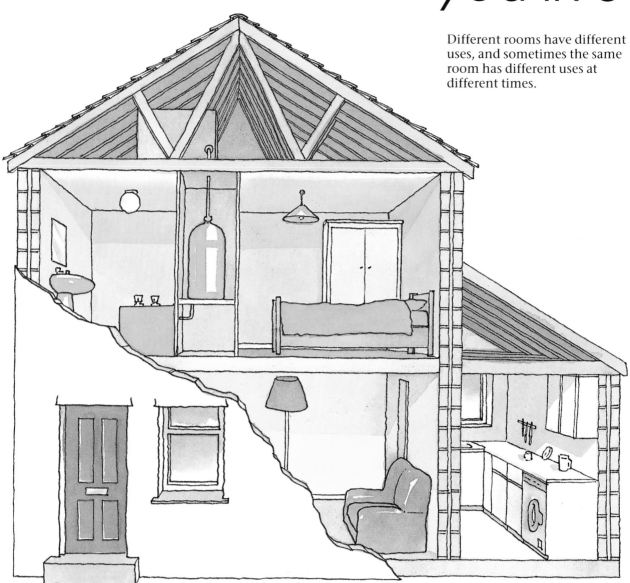

The kitchen may be where you prepare food and also where it is eaten. The lounge may also be the dining room and where you watch TV. The bedroom may be where you work as well as sleep. The bathroom may be the only place where you get to be alone and think.

Do you think your home is well designed? For instance, if you live in a semi or a terrace can you get from the front to the back without having to go through the house? If you live in an upstairs flat with one door, is there a fire escape?

How much time do you spend in each room during the day?

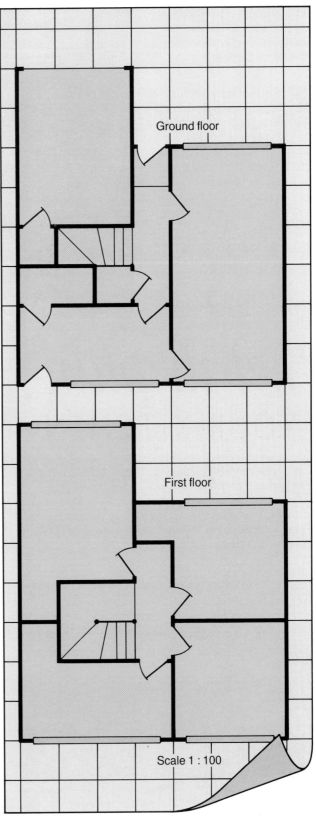

Ground floor

First floor

Scale 1 : 100

1 A ground plan of your home might help to identify any design faults. How would you improve things?

2 Look at these different colour schemes in the same room. They give totally different effects and feelings to the room. You could experiment with changing colour schemes to brighten a dull room, or make a bare room look cosy. Read the sections on colour and texture before you start (pages 96–99).

• D A T A   F I L E •
Drawing plans

The kitchen is probably one of the busiest rooms in the home, and needs the most careful planning.

No matter what size your kitchen is, it never seems big enough (Perhaps you might like to consider ways in which you could make your kitchen at home seem bigger.)

Kitchen A

'Let us plan,
YOUR KITCHEN'

Kitchens come in all shapes and sizes. Many organisations and business such as department and furniture stores provide information about kitchen design. Your local large DIY store may also have some kitchen plans. Here are some ready-made plans to give some ideas for creating your own.

Kitchen B

Kitchen C

I The symbols shown here represent some of the different tables, appliances and units, etc. that people have in their kitchens. Use these to redesign a kitchen layout for yourself using one of the floor plans shown. You may find it helpful to list all the different activities that go on in your kitchen at home or at a friend's. When you have done this, imagine that you are going to make a simple meal – beans on toast, boiled egg, or a cup of tea. What amount of walking did you have to do between the different parts of your design? Can you redesign your kitchen layout to reduce this amount of walking?

Plan A

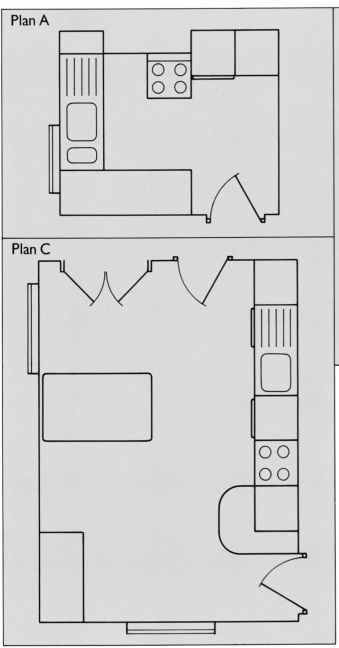

Plan B

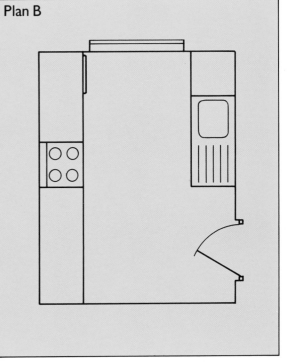

Plan C

A lot of research has been done on movement within kitchens. Kitchen designers concentrate on movement between three major items – the cooker (hob), fridge and sink. Are these items close together on your kitchen plan? If not, think about why kitchen designers try to put them near each other. Use this as another starting point in your ideas for a kitchen design.

Your teacher will give you some floor plans for kitchens. Use one of these to produce a 3-D scale model of your kitchen plan in card or stiff paper. Model the different items in the kitchen – appliances, tables, cupboards, etc.

2 Kitchen design has changed dramatically over the past fifty years. You might look at the design of kitchens during the whole of this century. You could look at medieval, Elizabethan, or Victorian kitchens. Find out what tools and materials were used. Try looking at the adverts in old cookery books and magazines to start you off.

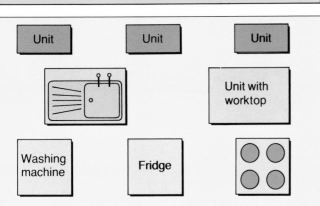

Unit	Unit	Unit
sink		Unit with worktop
Washing machine	Fridge	hob

• D A T A   F I L E •
Modelling techniques
Fit for people

There are many hazards in a kitchen. There are also many opportunities for design and technology to overcome these hazards.

Look at the pictures and discuss some of the problem areas. What projects could you tackle in an attempt to provide solutions? Keep notes of your ideas in your folio for future projects.

Many accidents occur in the kitchen. Find out about the different types of accidents that could happen. Certain age groups are more at risk than others. Find out about the hazards that the very young or elderly face in the kitchen. Try your local fire brigade, or perhaps the ambulance service. They may have an open day. You could write to ROSPA, the Royal Society for the Prevention of Accidents, to see if they have free literature.

S·A·F·E·T·Y
IN THE KITCHEN

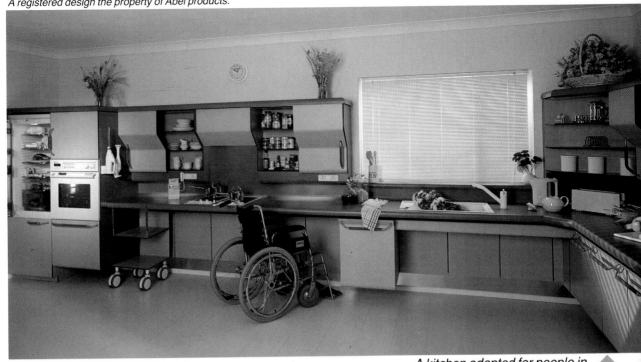

A kitchen adapted for people in wheelchairs

The shape of taps, door handles and light-switches, for instance, may need redesigning. Gather together a collection of items from the kitchen. Study them carefully and use this as the beginning of a product analysis. (If you need further help go to pp100, Around the house – product analysis.)

Keep a note of the results of your discussion and research in your folio to refer to when you start to tackle product design (pp 102–3).

Kitchens are dangerous places for able-bodied people. Handicapped people face even bigger problems. Their difficulties depend on the type of handicap. Some people have problems holding, reaching or turning things in the kitchen. You may know someone who is handicapped. Get them to tell you about their difficulties. How can you help to make life easier for them? You may be able to make devices that lift, switch, pull, push, twist or turn.

• D A T A   F I L E •

Fit for people
Disability information

91

YOUR
Bedroom

Imagine you are moving into a new house. Here's your chance to have a say in what your room might look like.

Think first of a bedroom you already know, perhaps your own, or a friend's:

- What type of furniture does it have?
- Does it have a wardrobe? Is it built in or moveable?
- Is the bed right for you?
- How about the colour scheme or use of pattern?

Now think of your room in the new house:

- Where would your bed fit?
- Will you have a fitted wardrobe and cupboards, or freestanding units?
- What carpets or rug patterns would suit the room?
- What colour scheme would you like?

Find out about:

- curtains, carpets, rug colours and patterns
- wallpaper designs and colours
- colours of paints
- types of paint and finish (matt, gloss, etc.) and where to use them
- ranges and styles of furniture.

Use catalogues, magazines, books and any other information sources to give you ideas for your bedroom designs.

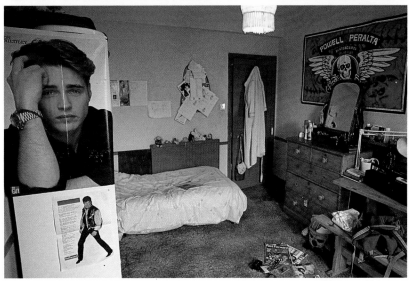

1 Draw a 2-D plan of your new bedroom. Your teacher may be able to give you some graph paper or squared paper.

Using your 2-D plan, cut out paper shapes to scale to represent the furniture in your room. Use this as another starting point in your ideas for the design of a bedroom. Think about the movement between different parts of the bedroom – bed to wardrobe, desk to bed, desk to window etc., that could take place. If you plan to have your own TV and music centre in your new room they need to be near sockets. These things all influence where the different items of furniture would go. You could then develop your flat 2-D plan into a 3-D scale model.

2 You may want to redesign your present bedroom, or your part of it – if you share with a sister or brother. What changes would you make?

3 You may like to create a scale model of just one corner of your bedroom.

Read through the next few pages on colours and textures for ideas for your project.

PERSONALISING

You might want to personalise your space – make it say something about your personal interests, or create a feeling or mood – by making a wall-hanging, an appliqué cushion, or a soft sculpture. Try sketching some initial ideas, thinking about:

- the bits and pieces you might have available
- the mood or feeling you wish to create
- the use of colour.

You may wish to consider how colour, texture and your personal hobbies can be used to enrich the designs of wallpapers, curtains, cushions, pillows, bedspreads or floor cushions for the bedroom you may have planned on page 92.

YOUR SPACE

Start to generate design ideas from a collection of things to do with your hobbies – pictures of footballers, TV personalities, pop or film stars. Your theme could be based on a collection of your favourite bits and pieces – a toy, a game, a medal or trophy, a musical instrument – anything will do as long as it gives you ideas for patterns.

One way to begin could be to fill a clear plastic container – a jar or bag – with some small objects. They could be from the list of collections above. They could have a common theme or be quite random. The idea is that this jumble of objects may spark off ideas for patterns.

Don't concentrate on single items in your collection but look for patterns, shapes, forms and colours. These may come about as many objects in the collection twist and tangle together. Try using a range of artists' materials – crayons, coloured pencils, felt tip pens, etc.

Before you make any final decisions you could make up a sample board. This is shown on page 97.

What about starting with the wall? Will you have painted or papered walls? Do you like patterned wallpapers? You could design your own, using pictures or patterns that reflect your personality. How will you come up with original and different designs? Where will you get your ideas? Bear in mind that colours can look very different in daylight and artificial light.

• D A T A   F I L E •

Artists materials
Textures
Using the natural environment

COLOUR MY WORLD

Colour plays an important part in our life. We are all affected by the colour of something. It could be the colour of our friends' clothes, the colour of a room, the colour of objects. Colour can create moods and atmospheres. Blue colours feel cold and reds feel warm. Bright colours give a sense of life and excitement; pastel colours can give a feeling of peace and serenity.

Which colours would you associate with:

| cold | warm | sad | angry |

| healthy | peaceful | confused |

Look at the cartoons and suggest colours for the moods of the people you see.

The colour circle is made up of twelve **hues** (or colours). A **tint** of each hue is made by mixing the hue with white. A deeper **shade** is made by mixing the hue with black. (The word 'shade' is used to describe the depth or degree of colour.) Remember that colours can look very different in daylight and artificial light.

Here are some short activities which could help you to understand how colour can create different effects.

1 You can experiment with matching colours by using the 'circle and square' arrangement. Place a red disc on a square of yellow, violet, blue and green in turn. Which seems cool and which seems warm?

Place the same sized discs on a yellow and blue square in turn. What effect do you notice? Which effect looks further away?

2 Look in magazines and other sources for pictures which give a warm feeling. Cut these out and stick them on a larger sheet to make a 'warm collage'. You could do a similar one to make a 'cold collage'. Look carefully at the colours in each of these collages. Are they noticeably different?

3 Coloured tissue papers can create a particular feel. Try making patterns by arranging certain shapes in various ways.

Before you make any final decisions you should make up a sample board. This should contain some of your ideas: paint samples, coloured materials, swatches, etc. Look at them at different times of the day – in sunshine and in shade, in bright artificial light. Do the colours reflect the mood you want to create?

You might want to find out what is meant by the following terms:

| pigments | primary colours | secondary colours |

| tertiary colours | neutral colours |

| complementary colours |

• D A T A   F I L E •
Artists materials
Textures

The natural world can also stimulate many ideas for colour and texture. All of these have inspired artists and designers:

- spiders' webs
- tree bark or branches
- moving water
- reflected light patterns
- a collection of shells
- pebbles or rocks

Try to capture an idea from nature by taking a wax rubbing.

Textured surfaces reflect light differently, just as different colours do, and this needs to be considered when making your choice of fabric, paint or other material.

Textures

Matt surfaces, such as a shaggy rug or a brick wall, absorb light – making their colours look dark and rich.

Shiny surfaces, such as gloss paint and wallpaper, reflect more light – making them appear brighter and paler.

Texture can emphasise the style and mood of the room. Shiny textures give a room a modern look; richly textured surfaces of wall-hangings, woven rugs or batik fabrics can create a warmer, ethnic atmosphere.

Here are some activities which could help you to understand how texture can create different atmospheres.

Dyeing and printing your own fabrics using natural materials and dyes.

Weaving as a means of decoration, using threads of different thicknesses or strips of different fabrics.

Tracing the origins of the fabrics of other countries – in particular the history or folklore that lies behind their design.

• D A T A   F I L E •

Artists materials
Textures
Using the natural environment
Printing techniques

AROUND THE HOUSE

Look at some objects found around the house that have been made or manufactured. These are called artefacts. Every one of these items has been designed.

lights
shelving
tables
curtains
spades
kitchen equipment
bathroom accessories
chairs
taps
wallpaper
flower pots
bowls
cups
knives, forks and spoons
carpets
vacuum cleaners
ornaments

Keep notes as you discuss some of these questions.

- Why have these things been made?
- Why have they been designed in the way they have?
- What materials have been used to make them?
- Why have these materials been chosen?
- Why is it the shape it is – decoration, function?
- Do you like the colour, shape, feel, texture?
- Does the object do the job it was intended for?
- Does it represent good value for money?
- How could these be designed differently (or better)?

PRODUCT ANALYSIS

Look at household objects from other times – the early part of this century, or the fifties for instance. You might like to look at the development of the telephone as a household item over the past seventy-five years – or what about the design of cutlery or door handles! What things have influenced the design over the years? How could you improve it?

Household items in other cultures may be dramatically different from those you are familiar with. Find out about household items from other times and other cultures.

• D A T A   F I L E •

Evaluating
Fit for people
Fair testing
British standards

AROUND THE HOUSE -

Look at the different types of lights that you might find around the home.

Discuss and keep notes about what you find out.

- How many lights do you have in your home?
- Where are the lights positioned?
- What power are the lamps (wattage)?
- What is their use:
  to illuminate?
  to decorate?
  to create an atmosphere?
  to prevent burglary?

PRODUCT DESIGN

You might like to find out what people use lighting for by conducting some market research. You need to think very carefully about the type of questions you want to ask as the information will help you to make decisions about the sorts of lights people want. Carry out your first survey amongst your friends or the whole class. If you need further information try asking members of your family and their friends.

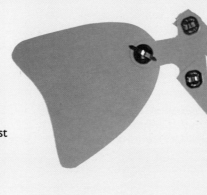

The picture shows a model of an adjustable lamp. However, it has some design faults. Sometimes it's only by making a model that we can see where the design fails. Your teacher will give you a sheet containing the parts of the lamp.

- Glue the shapes onto stiff paper or card.
- Cut out the shapes that make up the lamp and the connectors.
- Put the adjustable lamp together using paper fasteners.

- Find out why the lamp doesn't work and design a better one.
- Now evaluate your design by comparing it with a real anglepoise lamp.

You could make a prototype of your design using a more resistant material – wood or plastic for instance.

Use this activity to help you make decisions about types of lights or lighting systems you may be thinking of designing.

THINK ABOUT

flexibility   rotation   stretch   size of bulb

area of sweep   possible materials

covering of base   reflectability   colour

reach   shape of cone   area of illumination

grip of base   heat output   cable use (routing)

stability   function of joints

• D A T A   F I L E •
Evaluating
Research techniques
Joints

Sometimes a house just isn't big enough. Growing families, or growing hobbies, need more room.

Why do people/families need more room at home?
Is it for:

a larger family
extra space for grandparents
an extra workroom or utility room?

What changes do people make to their homes? Look around your community or area. Is anything being built on your way to school?

How many different types of extensions are built? Look for extra bedrooms, another garage, conservatories, extended kitchens or loft conversions perhaps. What seems to be the most popular type of alteration or extension?

'GOING-OUT ▶

Mrs and Mr B. Larger run a small building firm. They specialise in home improvements and extensions. They are planning on producing a range of materials such as calling cards, newspaper advertisements and a brochure of types of extensions including pictures of work already completed.

Can you help them?

ADDING ON

GOING-UP ▶ GOING-IN'

Start by looking through *Yellow Pages* for some firms that specialise in loft conversions or extensions.

How are their advertisements set out? Do they advertise in the local paper? Someone may be able to come to your school and talk to you about their business. They may be able to bring with them examples of their work including photographs.

• D A T A   F I L E •

Graphics

There are many different types of roof shapes. Here are a few.

The traditional design for Britain is the pitched roof.

The beams in the attic holding up the roof may be different shapes and patterns.

A typical roof structure might look like the diagram here.

You may find some different types of roofing material at your local DIY store. Look at the material. How much does it weigh? Is it very dense?

You could model a simple roof structure.
What material will you use? It needs to mimic the way real materials behave.

Perhaps you could use balsa wood strips for the rafters and battens. You could make cardboard slates and raid the kitchen for the ridge tiles. Dry spaghetti is a valuable material to use here. It mimics wooden beams and steel girders very well. It is reasonably strong and easily stuck together with polystyrene cement.

Try loading this structure to represent the weight of the roof. The weight would have to be distributed evenly.

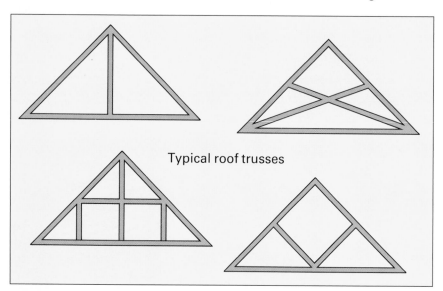

Typical roof trusses

A ROOF OVER

What effect would the weight of snow have on the roof structure? How would you test this?

Test your design for possible weak points. How could the roof be strengthened against storms and high winds? What would your new design look like?

Try to obtain an estimate for the relative costs of the different designs for your roof structures. How much do the different materials cost? How much do you need? What are the labour costs? Is the cheapest roof the best one to build? (It may be the lightest too.)

YOUR HEAD

•<u>DATA FILE</u>•

Structures

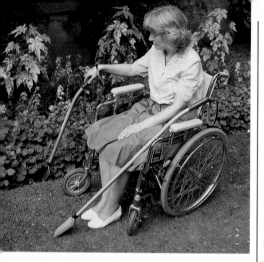

The garden is an extension of the home. As gardening becomes increasingly popular more and more garden centres are opening throughout the country. Providing for gardeners' needs has led to a rapidly growing industry in this country.

IN THE garden

People enjoy having a garden for many reasons:

- the pleasure of growing flowers and shrubs
- the pleasure of growing vegetables and fruit
- to provide space for growing children and their needs
- to have space to entertain
- to provide an environment to attract insects, birds and other forms of wildlife
- to make a more pleasurable environment.

Many disabled people enjoy gardening and gardens can be designed to cater for their needs. Some garden tools have also been designed for people with a range of disabilities.

Birds are fairly easy to attract into the garden. Find out what type of environment might attract such birds as:

robins, blue tits, finches, wrens, chiff-chaffs, swallows, thrushes, doves and blackbirds.

You need a bird book or an encyclopedia.

What sort of surroundings or nesting sites would attract resident or migrating birds?

Keep a record of your research in your folio to refer to later if you tackle the project on page 115.

Greenhouses come in all sorts of sizes and shapes. They are put to a variety of uses:

growing fruit and vegetables

growing exotic plants

growing seeds for summer bedding plants

over-wintering outdoor plants.

Attracting wildlife to the garden is a good way of controlling pests. Wildlife can also bring extra colour and activity into the garden.

Maybe you have no space in your garden for a greenhouse. Designs for smaller greenhouse-like structures might be more suitable in a small garden.

Many plants need a carefully controlled environment in the greenhouse. The temperature, moisture or light levels may need to be checked and action taken when things are not right.

The next section looks at controlling the growing environment with the help of technology.

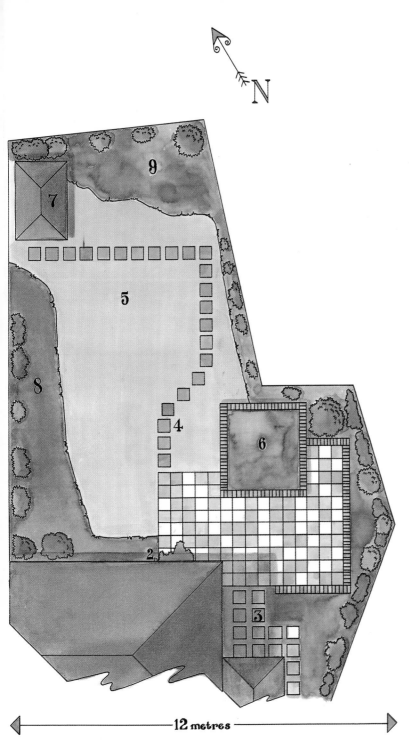

You may want to look at garden tools that could be used by both disabled and able-bodied people.

What type of garden games do you enjoy?

What equipment do you use?

Space for games might be difficult in a small garden. How could best use of the space be made?

The picture shows a small town garden which needs to be well planned if the owners are to get the most from it.

1 They like to grow indoor plants.

2 There are plants growing up the side of the house facing north.

3 This small area is in almost permanent shade.

4 Paving stones on the lawn provide a dry path in winter.

5 Keeping the lawn green and weed free is a perennial problem.

6 Access to a raised bed is across a paved area from the house.

7 Garden tools need to be safe and tidy.

8 This acidic bed – through use of peat-based fertiliser – can support only a few kinds of plants.

9 This heavy clay bed is due to mixing-in of thin top-soil layer with clay sub-soil.

Each of these areas presents its own problems and opportunities for design and technology. What kind of people would have a garden like this? Always keep the people you're designing for in mind.

Suppose they wanted this garden to give all-year-round colour. How would you help them?

You could start by looking at the month-by-month section of a gardening book, or finding some gardening magazines. If you plan to plant trees, find out how long they take to grow and how tall they grow.

Gardeners have many needs. Some of them are:

- making sure the soil is in good condition
- keeping the growing area weed free
- keeping pests under control.

Commercial gardeners grow both for profit and for other people's pleasure. Their needs may be different from someone growing plants in a greenhouse in the back garden. Garden centres and shops need to be kept well stocked with produce.

Many plants these days are mass produced – from radishes to roses. Visit your local nursery and make some notes on how commercial growers control their environment. Do they use electronic systems?

Plants grown on a production line basis in large quantities need to be carefully monitored. Electronic systems are very useful in keeping a watchful eye on what is happening in the garden or greenhouse.

g IN THE garden

Controlling THE *Environment*

A simple system for monitoring the temperature in the growing area might be:

| Monitor temperature | → | Process information | → | Act on results |

Electronically this could be:

| Temperature sensor | → | Control system | → | Fan blowing cold air |

Many systems allow you to feed electronic signals into the system using remote sensors. Try out some of your design ideas for remote sensors. Use information from the Datafile.

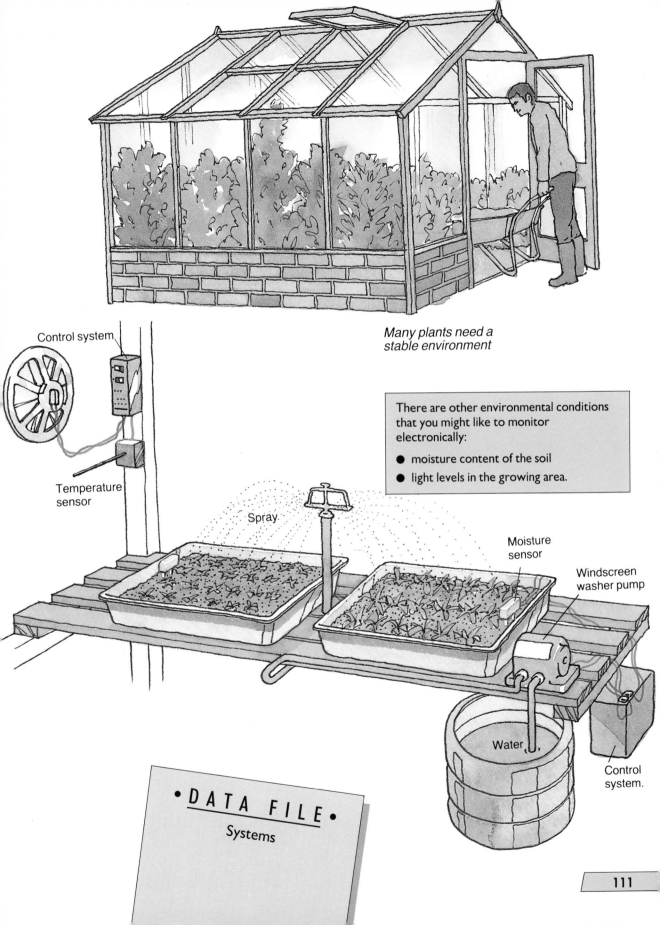

Control system

Temperature sensor

Many plants need a stable environment

There are other environmental conditions that you might like to monitor electronically:

● moisture content of the soil
● light levels in the growing area.

Spray

Moisture sensor

Windscreen washer pump

Water

Control system.

• D A T A   F I L E •
Systems

g IN THE arden

Electronic systems can also be used to monitor wildlife activity in the garden. You might like to sense when birds arrive to feed at a birdtable, or when hedgehogs or foxes move about the garden. The type of sensor you design will need to fit into the situation unobtrusively, i.e. without the animal sensing the sensor.

In some cases you may wish to detect the movement of people. They may be disturbing the animal environment.

Many ideas for sensors are found in the Datafile.

Detecting animal movement

• DATA FILE •
Electronic systems
Sensing

GARDENS FOR Special purposes

Imagine that the house on page 109, with its small garden, has now been bought by new owners.

They could be a family with young children, or keen birdwatchers, or an elderly couple.

These different owners all have very different needs. Many design and technology projects come about because someone else tells you of their needs.

You may often be given a problem to solve.

The three design challenges on this page could help these new owners.

Before you start, think about what other information you need to plan the garden. Where will you find the information? Will you need to do any market research by means of a questionnaire? Are there any organisations who can help you by sending free literature?

Always keep in mind the people you are designing and making for.

Situation 1

I A local firm of play equipment for parks and gardens is looking for some new designs of playhouses and climbing frames. This firm has sent a letter out to all schools in your area asking for new ideas. Develop a range of climbing frames, slides, play-houses and raised walkways for 4 to 10 year olds for use in small gardens.

(Use art straws, card and string or similar materials for your early ideas. Develop prototypes of your final designs using more resistant materials.)

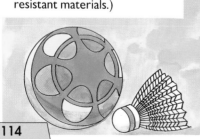

Situation 2

2 Imagine that the Worldwide Fund for Nature has recently announced a new competition. They want to look at ways of attracting wildlife, especially birds, into different types of gardens – inner city, suburban, countryside, etc.

Situation 3

3 Your local garden centre has asked the class to design a small scented garden for the blind and visually handicapped which they plan to construct at the centre. You could use the garden on page 109 as the basis for your design. The Royal National Institute for the Blind provides blind gardeners with a range of helpful hints and tips. Blind or partially sighted gardeners may wish to grow the same plants as sighted people. Keeping down the weeds can be especially difficult.

• D A T A   F I L E •
Presentation techniques
Modelling techniques
Fit for people

Bits and bobs

Many people make their own garments. They do this to be individual. It can also save a lot of money! If you make your own clothes you may be left with a wealth of scraps of materials, threads and notions. Notions are bits and bobs of different items – buttons, fastenings, tapes, ribbons, threads, etc.

Look at the pictures showing different types of scraps. Choose one of these and suggest how it could be used sensibly.

Organise a collection of scrap fabric, thread, beads and bits and bobs within your school. What sort of items would be most useful? How can you be sure people will bring in what you need? A poster requesting help from everyone in school might help.

Once the collection is complete you will need to sort the scraps into groups. Think of ways of using up these items:

● decoration of an item to personalise it
● a collage picture depicting your interests or hobbies
● an appliquéd cushion for your bedroom
● textile gifts for birthdays or celebrations
● soft toys or dolls in costume
● soft sculpture, tidy boxes or containers.

Collect as many ideas as you can.

A NEW *LOOK*

What do you need?

- Scraps of materials of the same weight
- Pins and sewing needles
- Sewing threads
- Basic pattern shape of the finished item

Design your own selection of matching items for the kitchen. Choose any one of these and produce a paper pattern. Don't forget to add the seams and joints to your paper pattern designs.

Look at fabric items used in the kitchen. Are any of these suitable for making out of patchwork?

Investigate:

- how a template for patchwork is made
- the different shapes used for patchwork
- how the patchwork material can be made into items.

Once you have finished your investigations you could design and make up your own piece of patchwork material and then use it to make one of the kitchen items.

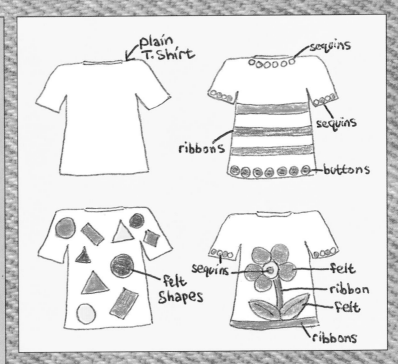

As well as being used for household articles, patchwork has at times been used to decorate clothing or for making an article of clothing itself.

By adding decoration to clothes we can change their appearance and also strengthen them should we wish.

We can apply decoration straight onto the garment or by wearing decorative additions – belts braces, buttons and buckles.

Choose a garment you have that you wish to re-vamp. Sketch some ideas of the ways in which you could add to or change the appearance of that garment.

Decide on the final choice for your design.

Before doing anything else it will be useful for your final evaluation if you take a photograph of the garment before you carry out any alterations.

You may wish to consider accessories to go with an outfit – gloves, hats, bags, scarves and decorated shoes. Design these to add to or complete your favourite outfit. Suggest the colours and materials you might use.

Give thought to the bits and bobs available and the need for durability – especially if the garment is frequently in the wash. This will not only influence the materials you will use but also the method of attaching the design to the garment.

You should also think about the skills and equipment necessary to carry out your design.

• D A T A   F I L E •

Making templates
Patchwork shapes

TRAVEL

We live in an age of travel. Going places is part of everyday life. For some this means going for a walk in the country, for others it means flying to the other side of the world.

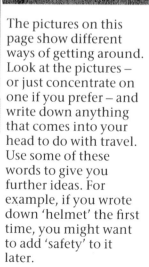

The pictures on this page show different ways of getting around. Look at the pictures – or just concentrate on one if you prefer – and write down anything that comes into your head to do with travel. Use some of these words to give you further ideas. For example, if you wrote down 'helmet' the first time, you might want to add 'safety' to it later.

Travelling and transport raise some important issues to do with the environment. Finding solutions may not be easy as you will need to take account of different people's views and opinions.

The desire for greater travel worldwide conflicts, for example, with the fear that some natural environments will become commercialised and changed or damaged beyond repair.

Discuss the issues raised by these conflicts of interest.

▶ 'We like to get out to the countryside at the weekend and breathe some fresh air.'
(City dweller)

▶ 'Cheaper air travel has brought exotic holiday spots within the reach of many.'
(Holiday brochure)

▶ 'I need my car to travel around and anyway, I get paid 20p per mile to use it.'
(Car sales representative)

▶ 'We can't cope with the cars bringing in the tourists.'
(Parish Council Chairman)

▶ 'Pardon?'
(Resident of Staines, near Heathrow Airport)

▶ 'I always take the bus. If everyone used public transport the roads would be less crowded. It would help to save the world's supply of fossil fuels.'
(Green Party voter)

Make notes on these discussions for your folio. See if you can use the ideas in future projects. You might also like to look at the environmental issues raised on page 40.

• DATA FILE •
Brainstorming

Out & about

Town and city pavements can be very busy places in the morning and evening rush hours. Think about the journeys you make on foot – to school, to the shops, to see a friend. Suppose you are coming home across a busy road in the dark. Just because the lights of a car are pointing straight at you doesn't mean the driver has seen you.

What can be done to improve road safety for pedestrians? Look at the entrance to your school or at busy street corners. Do they have safety barriers?

1 Many people wear special clothes so that they can be seen more easily when it's dark or nearly dark. For example, young children wear reflective bands on their arms and clothes. Sensible cyclists, too, wear brightly coloured clothes, often with reflective strips or bands.

Design some more ways of using reflective tape to make people safer in the dark. The tape doesn't have to be fixed to the people or their clothes. It can be fixed to anything that needs to show up well at night.

2 On your way to school, unless you live deep in the country, you probably pass street advertisements in a variety of forms in shop windows, on the sides of lorries or buses, on walls or on giant hoardings. What are they trying to sell? Are they eye-catching or have you often passed them without noticing what they said? Are they dangerous in that they could distract pedestrians or motorists while walking or driving along?

Can you design a hoarding advertisement that is eye-catching, but not enough to cause an accident?

What do you look at when you are travelling around by road? What things catch your attention – houses, the countryside, the wildlife, the different vehicles on the road, road signs, the style and shape of bridges?

If you are on a school or family outing you might want to break your journey for refreshments. Could the cafe or restaurant be made more comfortable? What is the state of the decoration? Is it light and airy, or is it a gloomy place?

What sort of maps do you or your friends or parents use to get about? Are these maps helpful enough? Is there enough information on the page? Is there too much information? How could they be improved?

What special needs do passengers on trains and ships have?

These are some of the topics we cover in this theme. Before you turn the page, discuss one or two of the ideas and work out what opportunities they present for design and technology. Keep your notes in your folio for reference when you come to plan further projects.

• D A T A   F I L E •

Graphics

ALONG THE WAY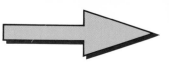

We are surrounded by signs along the way. They are used to tell us many things. Most signs give us a message as simply as possible. Some signs give a lot of information from a very simple, clear picture. Road signs are no exception to this. Road signs have to be clear and be easily and quickly understood.

Road signs are used to warn, inform, or give orders and directions. Here are a few road signs found in the Highway Code. What do they mean?

Some signs are warning signs. Some tell you what to do. How can you tell the difference?

New road signs are needed every now and again. What new road sign designs can you come up with? What new situations might they be used for? How would you find out how good your designs were?

Maps are very visual and vivid. Some are very detailed, yet easy to read. Some maps look cluttered. Some give you a lot of information with very little detail. You can buy a wide range of maps.

Different people need different types of maps. Hikers might need maps with a great deal of detail on them. Motorists may just need to know where the main roads and junctions are. Visitors to a museum may want to know where the main exhibition rooms or information points are.

What sort of maps might the following people need?

- Tourists in a cathedral city wanting to go out in the evening for a meal and to explore on foot
- A family going out for a trip in the afternoon
- A business person going to a large city by car
- Some teenagers out cycling for the day

When would you use a map if you were:

in school
at home
in the country
in town

What sort of map might you need?

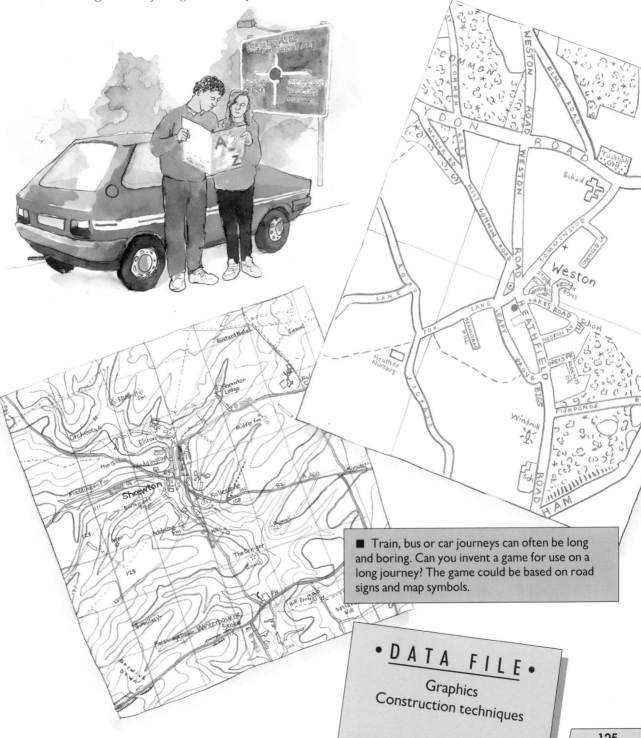

■ Train, bus or car journeys can often be long and boring. Can you invent a game for use on a long journey? The game could be based on road signs and map symbols.

• D A T A   F I L E •
Graphics
Construction techniques

When you're on a long car or coach journey somewhere don't you feel that you want to stop for a break every now and then for a meal or a drink, or just to go to the toilet? There are lots of places where different services are available to the traveller. The facilities provided are often quite mixed though. Standards vary. But you're not the only one on the road. Each day many different people are travelling for many different reasons:

- families going on holiday
- lorries delivering goods from one end of the country to the other
- businessmen and women
- coach drivers on long-distance tours
- taxi drivers
- cyclists
- motorcyclists.

What different things would some of these people want if they stopped for a break? You need to collect some information somehow. Would a questionnaire do? What other sources of information could you use – the AA, or RAC perhaps?

• D A T A   F I L E •

Presenting information
Modelling techniques
Nutritional guidelines

F A R E

Find out about the facilities available in some of these places near you:

- wayside cafe
- transport cafe
- roadside fast-food outlet
- public house or inn
- motorway service station
- country picnic area
- main road service station.

What facilities would you look for if you had to make a stop during a journey?

Here are some ideas which might be used as starting points for design opportunities. Take one of the settings in the picture. What kind of place is it? What sort of customer does it cater for? Try and identify exactly what needs to be done in each case:

1 to create a more pleasant eating environment, taking account of heating and lighting, furniture, colour and ventilation

2 to provide first aid or medical services

3 to provide a more multicultural range of foods given the opening up of the European market

4 to improve facilities such as toilets, washrooms, baby rooms and rest areas

5 to channel the flow of people through a cafeteria-style restaurant more efficiently

6 to provide non-smoking and smoking areas

7 to provide details of the nutritional value of fast-food on sale and give suggestions where necessary for more healthy meals

8 to provide adequate parking spaces for a range of vehicles.

A motor car is an artefact – a made thing, an object. It is also a system – or, more precisely, a collection of systems: the engine system, transmission system, braking system, exhaust system and so on.

Finally, a motor car is an environment – the seats, the trim, the fascia or dashboard are all designed to blend in and create a pleasant atmosphere.

Designing the environment

The environment within a car depends on a number of things:

- the type of car – saloon, sports car, hatchback
- the car model
- the user, or users – business traveller, exhibition organiser, family of seven
- their lifestyles and individual needs – baby seat, quadrophonic sound.

What else might influence the environment within a motor car?

The in-car environment depends upon who you are. It would be different for adults, children or babies. Different people have different needs.

You might like to consider design ideas to do with:

- seat covers
- steering wheel covers
- car gizmos, gadgets and gimmicks
- workclothes for car repairs
- gloves and jackets
- tools or torches
- anti-theft devices
- child seats

Some examples of these are shown in the pictures.

You could start a project by collecting some of the items shown, or pictures of them in catalogues, in order to do a product evaluation, which you should keep in your folio. The following questions could be used as starting points.

► Why has this been made?
► Why has it been designed in the way it has?
► What materials have been used?
► Why were these materials chosen?
► Why is it the shape it is – decoration, function, etc?
► Do you like the colour, shape, feel, texture?
► Does the object do the job it was intended for?
► Is it good value for money?
► Could it be designed better?

There are also the broader environmental issues to be considered when designing motor vehicles or designing for motor vehicles.

Does unleaded petrol contribute to the greenhouse effect?

How dangerous to health are exhaust pollutants like lead?

Are diesel engines cleaner?

How about electric cars?

Is gasohol a possible fuel?

How can CO and CO_2 emissions be cut down?

Should town planners be for, or against, the motor car?

Government transport policy – is there one?

Motorways or railways? – Or what?

Public or private transport?

You might need to take account of some of these issues when you are engaged in the process of designing. They may help with background information and influence the direction your designing takes.

• D A T A   F I L E •

Materials
Fair testing
Presenting information
Evaluating

CREATING
the image

Many road users use logos, emblems, trademarks or symbols that:

- advertise
- create an impression
- give information.

Look at the collection shown here.

A B T A

Express

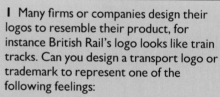

Successful logos, catch phrases or trademarks are immediately recognisable. They convey an image. Can you name some of the firms or companies that use these logos? What do they do or make?

Does the logo make you think of the product or the company? What comes into your mind when you see some of these logos or trademarks?

1 Many firms or companies design their logos to resemble their product, for instance British Rail's logo looks like train tracks. Can you design a transport logo or trademark to represent one of the following feelings:

- speed
- comfort
- safety
- warmth
- dependability.

2 Imagine that you are in one of the following businesses:

- home removals
- decorating
- parcel delivery
- household fabrics and furnishings
- public or private transport.

Try and design a logo or trademark that captures both who you are and what you sell.

Think about where you would display your logo. This might also influence your design. Logos are found in a variety of places:

- on clothes
- on sports cars
- on car accessories
- at service stations
- on the sides of buses and coaches
- on freight lorries
- on business vans and cars.

3 Suppose you are the manager of a chain of pizza restaurants. Part of the business is undertaken by a fleet of vans delivering pizzas at home. What sort of image do you try and create? Think about the vans, their drivers and the product you're selling.

Can you use this situation to design a logo, a slogan, an image or artefacts related to this particular business? The pictures show some of these ideas for graphic presentation. Use some of these together with your own designs.

• D A T A   F I L E •

Graphics

Designing for SAFETY

What makes a good car design?
If you were buying a car, what
would be important to you?

- comfort
- style
- speed
- economy
- colour

Whatever else cars are designed
for, they are designed to be
safe!

Audi Safety Systems

Rigid passenger safety cell

1. Procon-Ten pulls in the steering wheel in the event of an accident.

2. Procon-Ten tensions the front seat belts.

3. Front seats have been designed to prevent 'submarining' in an accident.

4. Bonded windscreens add to body rigidity and prevent the screens from coming out during an accident.

5. Seat belt mounts can be adjusted for height.

6. Side impact protection bars within the doors.

7. Seat mounted safety belt buckles for optimum occupant positioning.

8. Impact absorbing girders.

9. Impact absorbing materials on roof lining, dashboard & steering column.

10. Deformable energy absorbing body section.

11. Protected positioning of the fuel tank.

12. Self-stabilising steering.

13. ABS anti-lock braking system.

14. Front and four wheel drive.

15. Engine & drive line will collapse away from the passenger safety cell and not into it.

16. Rear belts allow for simple single-handed use.

17. Door pillar design spreads impact loads to the roof & floor to maintain passenger cell integrity.

18. Pedestrian injury risk reduced by flush door handles, integral rain channels, recessed wipers and plastic faced bumpers.

19. Galvanisation stops rust reducing body integrity and strength.

Vorsprung durch Technik

Car safety is always in the news, especially after a serious road accident. A great deal of testing is done on new car designs. The safety of the driver and passengers is top priority. Yet accidents still happen.

Car manufacturers go to great lengths to make sure that the occupants of their cars are safe. Crumple zones and protective shells work together to keep passengers safe. A difficult task a car designer faces is making the passenger compartment very strong while making the ends of the car absorb energy during impact.

Extra protection in cars usually means extra weight. Extra weight probably means that it uses more fuel. What other factors might influence the design of new cars? Car design is always a careful balance between opposing interests.

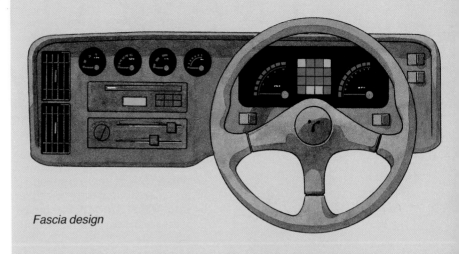

Fascia design

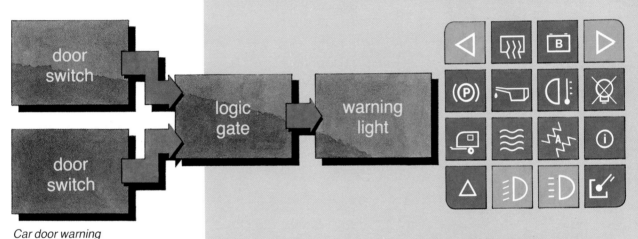

Car door warning system

AUTOMATIC SYSTEMS

1 In the teacher's guide is a development of a model car. Cut this out and put it together. Design a set of tests which could tell you how strong the car is. You will have to make a few of these models to test for collisions from the front, back and sides. Can you suggest ways to protect any occupants in the car? Make another model and build in your suggestions.

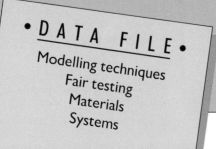

• **D A T A   F I L E** •
Modelling techniques
Fair testing
Materials
Systems

2 There are many automatic systems in cars. Many of these are to do with safety. Others give you information about the state of the car. Warning lights come on when the oil pressure is low, when the brake linings need changing, when the petrol is low in the tank or when the doors are not shut properly. Security warning devices are now fitted to many vehicles.

What other automatic warning devices are there in some vehicles?

You can model some of these systems using an electronic systems kit.

Use this system as a starting point for designing your own electronic system.

TRAVELLING
in comfort

Comfort for drivers and passengers is very important, and a great deal of research is undertaken into the design of seats for all sorts of types of transport.

The seat designer must bear in mind many things:

whom the seat is for

the size of the seat

the seat environment

the seat material

its structure.

Can you think of any others? List them in your folio to refer to later in your design project.

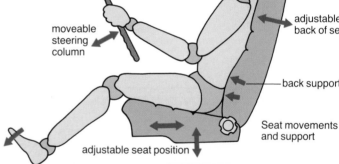

metal frame

cloth cover

foam interior

Typical car seat

A seat must be comfortable and safe for a wide range of people: short, tall, thin, fat, light, heavy. Look at the Datafile for information about ergonomics. One seat cannot suit everyone. Car seats are designed to cater for the majority of people. Probably about 90% of people would feel reasonably comfortable in any car seat.

adjustable head rest

adjustable back of seat

moveable steering column

back support

Seat movements and support

adjustable seat position

Pedal position for foot comfort

I How would you design a driver's seat? Any designs you come up with need to take account of the wide differences between people. You might like to start your research by doing a simple survey in your class. You could look at the variation in height, or weight, or shoe size or length of arm.

You could design and make some mannequins showing differences in body size and use these to help in your project designs and tests.

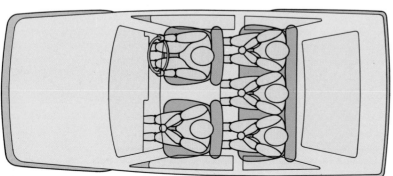

2 Try to get pictures of car designs from every decade of this century. Look carefully at them and at the ones pictured here. What has influenced the main design changes over the century? Which things haven't changed very much? Where do you think car design style will go in the future? Try to come up with your own futuristic designs.

1870s

1910

1920s

1900

1935 onwards

1980s

1960 onwards

2000 and beyond

• D A T A   F I L E •
Modelling techniques
Fair testing
Materials
Systems
Fit for people

THE LAUNCH

'Mayhem Motors' are to open a new garage in Havockam. They plan to introduce a new range of British saloon and estate cars, and the latest in the range is the seven-seater Clutterbus.

The managing director of Mayhem Motors is interested in an advertising campaign to promote the garage and the cars.

Walter Wall, their systems manager has been looking at the garage premises. He feels that a certain amount of rebuilding will have to be done before the garage opens.

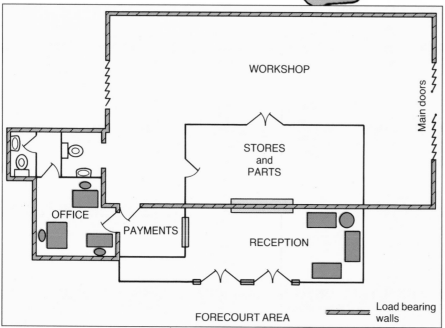

I The existing buildings do not lend themselves to a very efficient way of working. Some building work will be necessary to gain easier access to the different parts of the garage facilities.

The picture shows a simple layout of the existing building. Some of the walls are fixed (i.e. load bearing), but other walls could be shifted, taken away or new ones could be built.

You could use a construction kit to model the existing environment of the garage. This could be your starting point for redesigning the premises.

2 Walter Wall realises that other systems are needed for the smooth running of the garage.

You might like to think about:

● setting up a parts database
● creating a booking system for car repairs
● how to send reminders to customers that a car service is due
● how to send out bills and record payments received.

It might be possible for you to visit a large local garage and look at what systems they use before you go ahead with your own project.

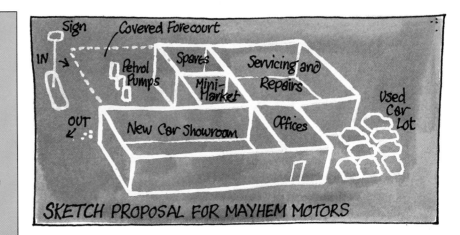

SKETCH PROPOSAL FOR MAYHEM MOTORS

3 A local advertising firm, Sellitt and Sellitt Ltd, have been asked to look after the Mayhem Motors advertising account.

You might like to design and make some advertising materials to promote the launch of the new garage and its products.

• D A T A   F I L E •

Systems
Information systems
Modelling techniques
Graphics

The advertising company

Elsie Dee, a leading light in Sellitt and Sellitt's promotions department, has presented a range of possibilities to Mayhem Motors.

First, she suggests an advertising campaign to launch a new car in newspapers, magazines, and on regional television.

Take a look at the car adverts in your local newspapers. How are the adverts set out on the page? Are they eye-catching? Do they contain any catch-phrases? Do they contain any real information? Do they want to make you go and find out more? Is what they are trying to sell clearly seen?

I How would you design a local media campaign to launch a new car?

Think about:

- the type of newspaper or magazine that Mayhem's adverts might appear in
- the type of people who might read them
- what you want to say, how to say it, and what information is essential.

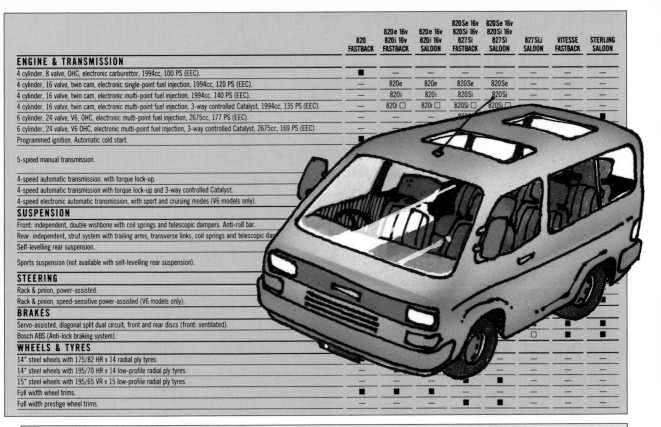

	820 FASTBACK	820e 16v 820i 16v FASTBACK	820e 16v 820i 16v SALOON	820Se 16v 820Si 16v 827Si FASTBACK	820Se 16v 820Si 16v 827Si SALOON	827SLi SALOON	VITESSE FASTBACK	STERLING SALOON
ENGINE & TRANSMISSION								
4 cylinder, 8 valve, OHC, electronic carburettor, 1994cc, 100 PS (EEC).	■	—	—	—	—			
4 cylinder, 16 valve, twin cam, electronic single-point fuel injection, 1994cc, 120 PS (EEC).	—	820e	820e	820Se	820Se			
4 cylinder, 16 valve, twin cam, electronic multi-point fuel injection, 1994cc, 140 PS (EEC).	—	820i	820i	820Si	820Si			
4 cylinder, 16 valve, twin cam, electronic multi-point fuel injection, 3-way controlled Catalyst, 1994cc, 135 PS (EEC).	—	820i □	820i □	820Si □	820Si □			
6 cylinder, 24 valve, V6, OHC, electronic multi-point fuel injection, 2675cc, 177 PS (EEC).	—							■
6 cylinder, 24 valve, V6 OHC, electronic multi-point fuel injection, 3-way controlled Catalyst, 2675cc, 169 PS (EEC)	—							
Programmed ignition. Automatic cold start.								
5-speed manual transmission.								
4-speed automatic transmission, with torque lock-up.								
4-speed automatic transmission with torque lock-up and 3-way controlled Catalyst.								
4-speed electronic automatic transmission, with sport and cruising modes (V6 models only).								
SUSPENSION								
Front: independent, double wishbone with coil springs and telescopic dampers. Anti-roll bar.								
Rear: independent, strut system with trailing arms, transverse links, coil springs and telescopic dampers.								
Self-levelling rear suspension.								
Sports suspension (not available with self-levelling rear suspension).								
STEERING								
Rack & pinion, power-assisted.								
Rack & pinion, speed-sensitive power-assisted (V6 models only).								
BRAKES								
Servo-assisted, diagonal split dual circuit, front and rear discs (front: ventilated).								
Bosch ABS (Anti-lock braking system).						□	■	■
WHEELS & TYRES								
14″ steel wheels with 175/82 HR x 14 radial ply tyres.						—	—	—
14″ steel wheels with 195/70 HR x 14 low-profile radial ply tyres.		—				—	—	—
15″ steel wheels with 195/65 VR x 15 low-profile radial ply tyres.		—			■		—	—
Full width wheel trims.	■	■	■	■		—		
Full width prestige wheel trims.	—			■	■		—	—

2 To back up your campaign you need to present some technical information. Here you might consider how to promote Mayhem's new release – the Clutterbus. You could include some information on environmental issues. Look back at page 40 onwards for some ideas.

Look at some magazines produced by the motor manufacturers for clues on how to present technical information.

3 Now the garage has been redesigned, a grand opening is planned to launch it. A wide range of possibilities was considered by Sellitt and Sellitt, the advertising firm. Some of these were:

● launch/opening lunch

● free gifts – travel pack – Mayhem hats – maps and games

● competition in local newspapers

● T-shirt designs.

You might wish to develop some of these ideas.

• D A T A   F I L E •

Graphics
Research techniques
Presenting information

PRODUCING THE GOODS

'Built by robots' has become a familiar phrase. Many of the things we see around us are mass-produced. From knives and forks to double-decker buses things run off the production line.

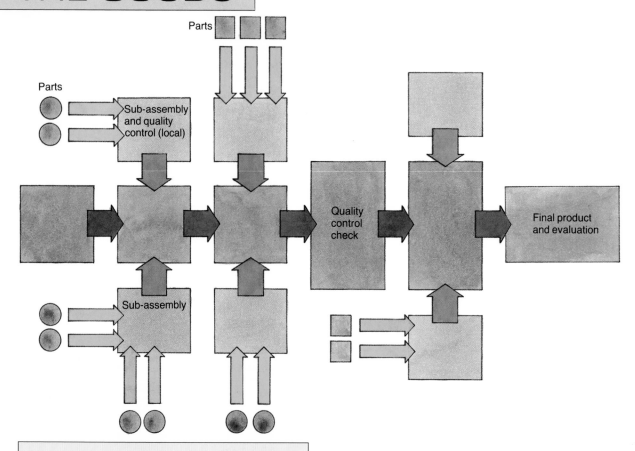

Parts

Parts

Sub-assembly and quality control (local)

Sub-assembly

Quality control check

Final product and evaluation

For many years a local toy manufacturer has been producing a range of small vehicles from its range of technical products. You wish to enter the toy market and produce a similar range. You intend to make these vehicles out of parts from a construction kit. The artefact could be a car, tractor and trailer, lorry, bulldozer, coach, or something similar.

You plan to set up a company to include:

● management team
● research team
● planning team
● design team
● team of workers to do the nitty-gritty hard work!
● team of quality control specialists
● marketing team.

Some people could be in more than one team.

You need to decide:

● what the item will look like
● how many components it is made from
● whether it can be made from smaller sub-assemblies
● whether the operatives need training
● how many people you need to assemble the item
● the cost of the item
● how to supply an adequate number of parts for assembly.

What other factors do you think need to be taken into consideration?

You should aim to produce a minimum of 25 items in any production run. Each item should be made from no more than 25 components.

During your production run look for any bottlenecks. Are there times when some of the workers do not have enough work to do? Are some people under too much pressure? You might also like to time your production run.

Discuss the activity amongst yourselves. Let everyone say how they feel. How could your production line become more efficient – either in making more items or taking less time, or in using less workers. What else might make your production more efficient? If necessary re-design your production line and try again. Is your new production line better than before?

1st run		
Vehicle number (Start clock)	Vehicle comes off production line sec/mins	Time to make each vehicle
1		
2		
3		
.		
.		
.		
23		
24		
25		
	Total time to make 25 vehicles is _____	Average time to make each vehicle is _____

Managers in industry have to make decisions like this every day. What might be the results of redesigning a production line? Would anyone be out of a job? Would anyone be doing less work and be paid less as a result? Would anyone be paid more for doing more work or different work?

You might like to look more carefully at the cost of making your vehicle and take into account:

    cost of components
    wages/salaries
    selling costs
    size of selling market.

Can you think of anything else you should take into account?

• D A T A   F I L E •

Systems
Management systems
Information systems
Production
Modelling techniques

AUTO MATE!

There may be some parts of the activity on pages 140–1 that could be automated. Making parts of a production line automatic also has many implications for the company and the people who work for it. What might these be?

I You might like to consider the use of a computer system to set up some simple situations that represent parts of a manufacturing process or production line.

Some things that you might like to think about are:

- counting how many objects pass by
- making sure that an object has the right weight
- checking the height of passing objects
- checking time intervals between operations
- sorting items by:
  - colour
  - height
  - weight

2 Meanwhile, back at Mayhem Motors, the team are looking at some ways of introducing automated systems into the garage. One system they would like to build into the workshop is a 'rolling road'. Rolling roads are used in garages to test the brakes of road vehicles.

Having some kind of battery operated car might be useful here. You might design a rolling road to test the performance of this vehicle.

You could start by using a motor as a dynamo. This would generate a voltage proportional to the speed of the rolling road.

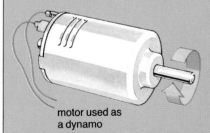

motor used as a dynamo

You don't have to use a computer system to do any of these activities. You could use an electronics systems kit. Mechanical systems could also be used to perform some of these functions.

LDR

You could also send pulses from a slotted opto switch to the computer to be counted. This would also give you an idea of how fast the rolling road was rotating.

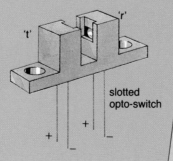

slotted opto-switch

The pictures give you some helpful hints.

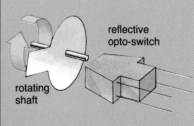

reflective opto-switch

rotating shaft

• D A T A   F I L E •

Control systems
Production
Fair testing
Materials

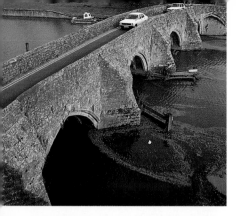

In the distant past travel was very restricted. Natural barriers such as mountains and rivers prevented people from moving around. Bridges enabled people long ago to begin to travel much further afield. Look at the different pictures of bridges from different times in history. Different times and cultures produce different styles of bridge. Their materials reflect these times and styles.

Getting

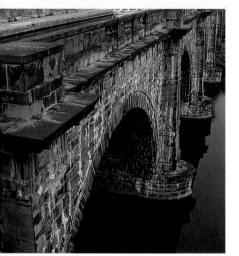

Find out:

what types of bridges these are

when they might have been built

why they were built

what they are built from.

Here are some pictures of more modern bridges.

Try to find out:

what they are called

where they are

what they are made from

why they were built

what the local conditions are like

over there

Use paper, card, paper straws, and similar materials to try out different bridge shapes. The bridges could be designed using some of the different sections and structures shown.

Think about tests that might be used to compare one design with another.

- What will you compare?
- What will you test?
- How will you do the test?
- Will it be a fair test?
- How will you record the test results?

Structures

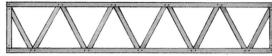
Warren truss

double Warren

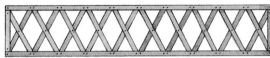
lattice

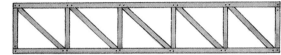
'N' or 'Pratt' truss

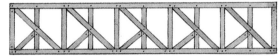
'K' or Pennsylvania truss

Sections

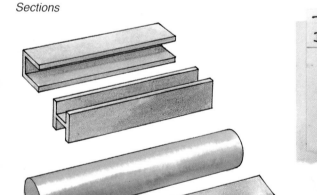

TYPE OF BRIDGE	WHAT I DID TO THE BRIDGE	WHAT HAPPENED TO THE BRIDGE

• D A T A   F I L E •

Fair testing
Materials
Structures
Modelling techniques

BRIDGES NEAR YOU

Look around at some of the bridges near your school. What types of bridges are they? How were they built? Are there any under construction? How are they being built? What are they being built for?

The type of bridge built depends upon various things:

- the ground being built over
- the span of the bridge
- the cost of materials
- the local environment
- local building materials.

What about bridges for pedestrians? There are many interesting designs and shapes of pedestrian bridges around. You could design a range of pedestrian bridges for use in a variety of different circumstances:

over a road or a river

over a roundabout

between blocks of flats

between different parts of a shopping centre.

TOO FAR

You are part of an expedition to discover the remains of the ancient civilisation of the Technitots. This group of people have left behind vast treasures. Whilst searching through the dense jungle you stumble across an enormous ravine. The sides of the ravine are a sheer drop of hundreds of metres. The ravine itself is only about 20 metres wide but the dense jungle grows right to the edge. You have only the simplest of materials – various thicknesses of rope, some cutting and sawing tools and some cloth.

Use cotton, string, thin card and fabrics to mimic these materials. Choose a suitable scale and design a rope bridge to carry you and your belongings over this ravine. The treasure awaits!

TAKING OFF

One of the most popular – the safest – ways of travelling is to fly. Millions of people in this country fly off to other countries for holidays or work. Some people fly from one end a this country to the other for work and pleasure.

There are many airports up and down the land. Some are large like Heathrow or Manchester, Prestwick or Shannon. Some are small, even down to the size of a field used perhaps by a local flying club.

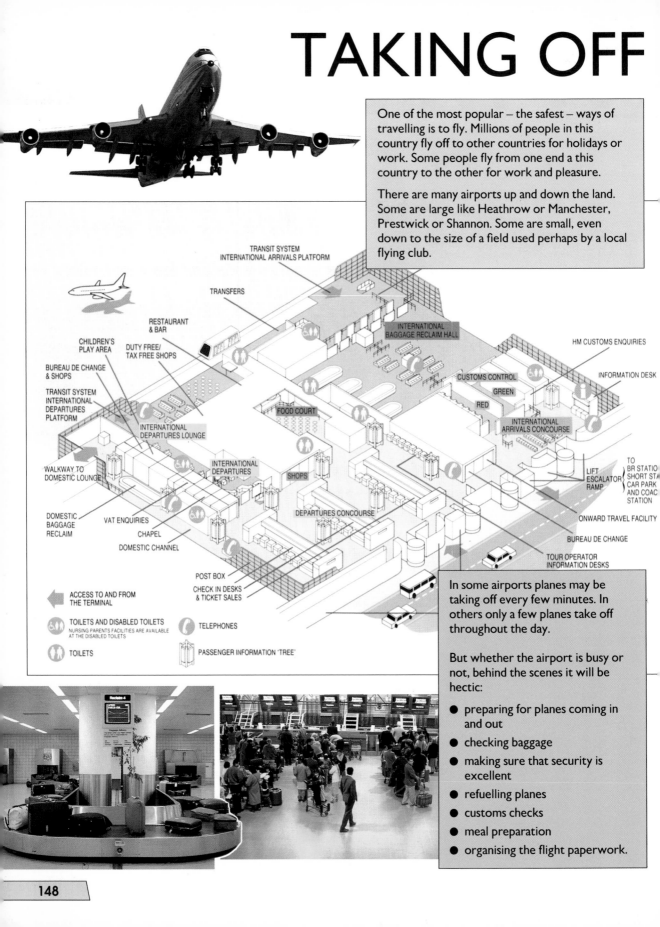

TRANSIT SYSTEM
INTERNATIONAL ARRIVALS PLATFORM

TRANSFERS

RESTAURANT & BAR

CHILDREN'S PLAY AREA

DUTY FREE/ TAX FREE SHOPS

BUREAU DE CHANGE & SHOPS

TRANSIT SYSTEM INTERNATIONAL DEPARTURES PLATFORM

INTERNATIONAL DEPARTURES LOUNGE

FOOD COURT

INTERNATIONAL BAGGAGE RECLAIM HALL

HM CUSTOMS ENQUIRIES

INFORMATION DESK

CUSTOMS CONTROL

GREEN

RED

INTERNATIONAL ARRIVALS CONCOURSE

WALKWAY TO DOMESTIC LOUNGE

INTERNATIONAL DEPARTURES

SHOPS

DEPARTURES CONCOURSE

DOMESTIC BAGGAGE RECLAIM

VAT ENQUIRIES

CHAPEL

DOMESTIC CHANNEL

POST BOX

CHECK IN DESKS & TICKET SALES

LIFT
ESCALATOR
RAMP

TO
BR STATIO
SHORT STA
CAR PARK
AND COAC
STATION

ONWARD TRAVEL FACILITY

BUREAU DE CHANGE

TOUR OPERATOR INFORMATION DESKS

ACCESS TO AND FROM THE TERMINAL

TOILETS AND DISABLED TOILETS
NURSING PARENTS FACILITIES ARE AVAILABLE AT THE DISABLED TOILETS

TOILETS

TELEPHONES

PASSENGER INFORMATION 'TREE'

In some airports planes may be taking off every few minutes. In others only a few planes take off throughout the day.

But whether the airport is busy or not, behind the scenes it will be hectic:

● preparing for planes coming in and out

● checking baggage

● making sure that security is excellent

● refuelling planes

● customs checks

● meal preparation

● organising the flight paperwork.

Some suggestions which might prove useful for projects are given here.

1 BAGGAGE HANDLING

You could design:
- simple ways of conveying baggage
- ways of sorting and checking passengers' baggage
- automatic doors
  - on lifts
  - between areas in an airport
  - main doors.

2 ENVIRONMENT

The environment that people have to wait in while waiting for their plane may need developing. In the restaurant area traditional national foods and those of an international flavour could be redesigned.

3 SECURITY SYSTEMS

You might want to design a warning system to detect unauthorised baggage. Your system might include some kind of metal detector.

4 INFORMATION SYSTEMS

An information system may need to be developed to keep passengers informed both pre-flight and in-flight.

5 ON BOARD

Once aboard the plane, there are other areas where you may be able to find ideas for projects:

airline uniforms

logos and corporate images

food preparation

seating arrangements

safety considerations

luggage storage

6 Shown here are some designs from the last 70 years. But what about the future? What will the planes of the future look like? Where will it all end?

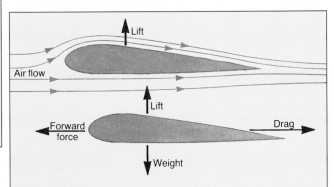

7 How do planes stay up in the air? Part of the answer lies in the design of the wings. Wing shapes vary depending upon the type of aircraft. You might like to design some new forms of wing shape. Test them to see how well they fly. Redesign them where necessary.

T ON THE RIGHT LINES

Trains, in one form or another, have been with us for over 150 years. In that time the engines, carriages and rolling stock have changed to make use of the latest technology. The railways today offer more than ever a tremendously exciting area for study and development.

Look at some of the pictures on this page. They are all concerned with aspects of rail travel. Study them carefully. You may find some opportunities and starting points for design and technology activities.

1 The historical side of the railways is very interesting. You may have had an opportunity to visit a railway preservation society and to see some old trains still running. Things were very different for the people who worked on the railways 50 or 100 years ago. How was the signalling done then? What was life like for a train driver or guard? What was passenger comfort like then?

3 Once on the train the passengers may still wish to be kept informed of where they are and what is going on. For long journeys the passengers may wish to read or hear about some of the sights along the way. Would they like piped music on the train or even piped poetry?

4 You might like a drink or a meal on the train. Carrying drinks from one carriage to another can be tricky. Non-spill cups could provide an answer.

2 This is a major railway station. People are waiting for the train to arrive. They need to know:

which trains are arriving and at which platform, which trains are departing and from which platform

the time

the destinations of the trains.

What other information do waiting passengers need? How could they obtain this information?

Train drivers also need to be kept informed. What information do they need?

5 What about specially packed food for that special occasion? It could be:

a trip on the Orient Express

a railway preservation society annual reunion

the opening of the Channel Tunnel

a train spotters' outing.

6 Some journeys can be very long. Some may last through the night. You may find that you suddenly need something – paper towels, toothbrushes, soap, hygienic baby wipes – is there a dispenser near by?

7 Perhaps there are games you can think of to play on trains.

8 A lot of time and effort goes into the design of the livery of trains. The uniforms of the drivers, guards, stewards, porters and other personnel all give a corporate image. The choice of colour scheme for the upholstery in the carriages also needs some careful thought. What about the colour scheme of the trains themselves?

9 What about the future? The Channel Tunnel link could open up new and exciting possibilities for rail travel into Europe. How will the railways respond?

Model of the proposed French terminal at Calais

• D A T A   F I L E •

Systems
Fit for people
Graphics
Food

ALL AT SEA

Britain is an island. We rely on shipping to keep the country going. Ships bring us the raw materials from which we make things. Ships bring us fuel. Ships bring us some of our foods. Ships bring tourists to the country. Ships take holiday-makers abroad. Ships take our exports away to other countries.

Hundreds of ships, large and small, visit our ports and harbours every day. You may live near the sea and watch the comings and goings in such a harbour.

Shipping offers a tremendously exciting area for study and development. Look at some of the pictures on this page. They are all concerned with aspects of sea travel and trade. Study them carefully. You may find some which offer opportunities and starting points for design and technology activities.

1 Until the Channel Tunnel is opened many people travelling to the continent will sail on a ferry.

Safety comes first in any means of travel. The various shipping companies must ensure that their passengers are safe. What ways are there of making sure that both people and their belongings are secure and protected?

2 Getting on and off ships can be time-consuming, especially if you have a car. There are systems for ensuring the rapid dispersal of passengers and cargo at ferries. It might be worthwhile looking into such a system.

3 Sometimes people get into difficulty at sea. It may be their own fault, it may be the weather, it may be a mechanical breakdown. What emergency services are there for dealing with people and ships in distress? What different types of systems are there for sending emergency messages? Many ships and ferries are equiped with lifeboats. These lifeboats contain equipment needed in an emergency.

Find out about the sort of equipment that might be needed. Can you think of anything else that might be needed?

4 Loading and unloading cargo at the harbour can take a great deal of time. To be economical ships need to be out at sea most of the time. The turn-around time in the harbour must be kept short.

5 Handling the cargo at the harbour must also be done efficiently. Containerisation has helped to achieve this. Find out about containerisation.

GALCONDA

• DATA FILE •

Systems
Fit for people
Graphics
Food

Aleph and Goma

Aleph and Goma and the rest of their group had arrived on the distant planet of Erifgol. Leaving the safety of their spaceship, the six intrepid travellers set out across the barren, lifeless, airless desert in their proto-skimmer. The craggy peaks of a mountain range loomed large on the horizon.

It was getting dark as they reached the foothills of the mountain range when they noticed some lights in the distance. No one had told them that the planet was inhabited. Aleph swung the joystick of the proto-skimmer to set them off looking for a vantage point.

In full protective clothes, Aleph led her crew out of their transporter. Keeping themselves well hidden, they used their telemagnifiers to see what lay before them . . .

Storywriter: Well, what do you reckon? Is that good enough to lead us off into a new series of adventures?
TV producer: Dunno, I'll have to think about it.
Storywriter: Well, let me know when you've decided 'cos the set designers will need at least six weeks.

Well, what do you reckon?

If you were asked to make the TV set or sets for this science fiction adventure series, what would you do?

— the story so far . . . .

Working in groups of about three or four you may wish to:

● write a short story using the beginning given here (or another beginning if you wish)

● focus on several scenes that would provide an interest point for the story

● use the idea of a storyboard to plan out this small part of the storyline (think about the set design and any special effects that might be needed).

The whole storyboard for an episode in the series might look like the design here.

Design one, two or at most three sets that could illustrate your chosen part of the story. You may want to use one set to illustrate a close-up of one scene.

Your group will have to make sure that the work you plan fits in with what has just happened in the story and what comes later.

STAR TECH

The planning stage

What will you need to make decisions about?

It could be such things as:

the scene or characters you intend to illustrate
the scale represented by the scene or characters
the physical size of the scene or characters
the materials you might need
the tools and equipment you might want to use
the availability of the materials
the timescale you have to work to
when things need to be made and be ready by . . .

. . . anything else?

You need to produce some kind of timeplan. This is because you will not want to waste time, energy or materials when you come to make your chosen scenes.

How do you think you could get a feel for the realism of the scene(s) that you have made? There are a variety of ways.

- The simplest way would be to use a card with a hole in it and look around the scene.

- You could use a 'point and click' camera to simply record the scene or a more sophisticated 35 mm camera with a macro lens to get close-up photographs. You may have some problems with focusing when you get in close.

- Use a small purpose-built periscope and look through it to get a close-up view of an obscured or hidden part of the scene.

Other things that you might like to consider are:

- the use of construction kits in making parts of the scene
- the use of parts of plastic modelling kits to represent some of the detail in some of the scene
- the use of thrown-away materials to make parts of the scene
- special lighting effects.

· D A T A   F I L E ·

Making a time plan
Storyboards

Glossary

aesthetic describing something thought to be pleasing to look at

advertising the way that we make something publicly known to other people

analysis breaking down a problem into simpler parts for investigation (*see* synthesis)

artefact an article which someone has made

brainstorming where a group of people produce ideas quickly, without stopping to discuss the details

budget amount of money needed or available, or a look at the money coming in and going out of a family or a company, for example

challenge in Design and Technology it means a sentence or paragraph which describes what you intend to do (*see* design brief)

commercial describing efforts which aim to make money or work to do with business or trade

communication information passed from person to person in words, signs or pictures

components parts of a whole

concept an idea

considerations things to think about

construction a frame, building or something made

consumer a person buying/using goods or services

context in Design and Technology it means a situation or place in which to explore a theme (*see* theme)

control a way of making things happen when and in the way that you want them to. It may also be thought of as how a system is kept working smoothly

criteria standards that something is judged by

cultures peoples who have developed a clear identity and way of life, e.g. North American Indians, Aborigines

data facts or information

database a set of facts or information that can be searched, altered and used

Datafile in the setting of this book, a place to look for information or facts

design brief a sentence or paragraph which describes what you intend to do (*see* challenge)

design proposal something which shows your design ideas

development in Design and Technology it means a flat (2-D) layout of something which can be made up as a model (*see* net)

electronics control system which uses miniaturised electrical circuitry in the form of microchips

enterprise adventure into business

environment our surroundings

ergonomics the study of how well people interact with their immediate environment

evaluate in Design and Technology it means to make judgements about designs and the way they were produced

factor something which may influence your decisions

feedback one way in which a system can be controlled

folio in the setting of this book, a record of your design activities

force something which may cause movement, e.g. twisting, bending, change of shape

form the shape of something

friction resistance to movement

function the use to which something is put

graphics the use of diagrams or drawings in design work

identify to notice or recognise something

implications what may be involved or might happen

inflation a rise in the level of prices

input something which goes into a system, e.g. goods sent into a factory, or an electrical signal (*see* output)

investigate to try to find out more about something

logo a picture or name which identifies a product or company

manufacture to make something, maybe in quantity

marketing the way goods are brought to sale. Marketing involves doing surveys, taking note of consumer needs and designing advertising campaigns.

materials media used in making, e.g. video, film, tape, food, pen, airbrush, paint, words, plastic, fabrics

mechanism moving parts working together to make something happen

modelling how to see ideas by making models. The models might be 3-D, computer simulations or mathematical predictions